Better Homes and Gardens

Timeless Recipes

Meredith® Books
Des Moines, Iowa

All of us at Meredith® Books are dedicated to providing you with the information and ideas you need to create delicious foods.

We welcome your comments and suggestions. Write to us at Meredith Books, Cookbook Editorial Department, 1716 Locust St., Des Moines, IA 50309-3023.

If you would like to purchase any of our books, check wherever quality books are sold or visit bhgbooks.com.

Our seal assures you that every recipe in *Timeless Recipes* has been tested in the Better Homes and Gardens® Test Kitchen. This means that each recipe is practical and reliable, and meets our high standards of taste appeal. We guarantee your satisfaction with this book for as long as you own it.

Pictured on front cover: Sweet-and-Sour Steak (see recipe, page 59)

Excerpted from the 2001 version of *Better Homes and Gardens® Easy Everyday Cooking.*

Timeless Recipes
Editor: Carrie E. Holcomb
Contributing Designer: Kimberly Zarley
Copy Chief: Terri Fredrickson
Contributing Proofreader: Jean Baker
Managers, Book Production: Pam Kvitne, Marjorie J. Schenkelberg. Rick vonHoldt, Mark Weaver
Publishing Operations Manager: Karen Schirm
Senior Editor, Asset and Information Manager: Phillip Morgan
Editorial and Design Production Coordinator: Mary Lee Gavin
Editorial Assistant: Cheryl Eckert
Test Kitchen Director: Lynn Blanchard
Test Kitchen Home Economists: Marilyn Cornelius, Juliana Hale, Laura Harms, Maryellyn Krantz, Jill Moberly, Dianna Nolin, Colleen Weeden, Lori Wilson, Charles Worthington

Meredith® Books
Executive Editor, Editorial: Gregory H. Kayko
Executive Director, Design: Matt Strelecki
Managing Editor: Amy Tincher-Durik
Senior Editor, Group Manager: Jan Miller

Publisher and Edior in Chief: James D. Blume
Editorial Director: Linda Raglan Cunningham
Executive Director, New Business Development: Todd M. Davis
Executive Director, Sales: Ken Zagor
Director, Operations: George A. Susral
Director, Production: Douglas M. Johnston
Director, Marketing: Amy Nichols
Business Director: Jim Leonard

Vice President and General Manager: Douglas J. Guendel

***Better Homes and Gardens®* Magazine**
Editor in Chief: Karol DeWulf Nickell
Deputy Editor, Food and Entertaining: Nancy Hopkins

Meredith Publishing Group
President: Jack Griffin
Executive Vice President: Bob Mate

Meredith Corporation
Chairman and Chief Executive Officer: William T. Kerr

Chairman and Chief Operating Officer: Stephen M. Lacy

In Memoriam: E. T. Meredith III (1933-2003)

DELICIOUS IDEAS FOR NO-FUSS MEALS!

Timeless Recipes offers satisfying solutions for everyday meal preparation. Filled with more than 120 family-pleasing recipes, this appealing collection includes innovative ways to prepare meats, poultry, and seafood as well as ideas for appetizers, soups, salads, vegetarian dishes, and desserts. Choose from tempters such as Herb-Pepper Sirloin Steak, Ruby-Glazed Chicken Breasts, Four Bean Enchiladas, Country Pear and Cherry Crisp, Chocolate Cream Cake, and more.

Don't waste a minute. Try some of these exceptional everyday dishes. They're perfect any time and every time.

Contents

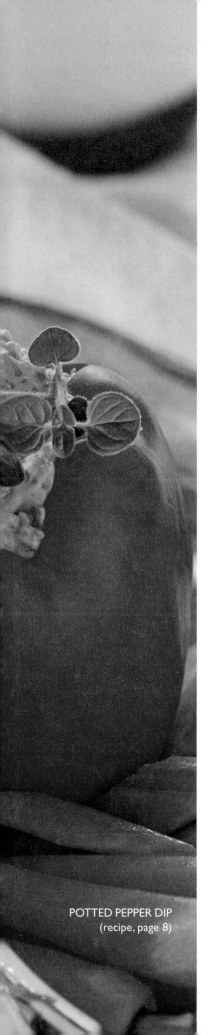

Appetizers
& SNACKS

Contents

Summer Fruit Salsa

The refreshing ingredients in this summer salsa pair well with grilled chicken breasts and fish steaks.

1 tablespoon lime juice
1 tablespoon plum or peach jam
½ cup finely chopped peach
½ cup chopped strawberries
½ cup finely chopped fresh pineapple
½ cup finely chopped plums
2 tablespoons finely chopped red onion
1 jalapeño pepper, seeded and finely chopped
  Dash ground cloves
  Jalapeño peppers, cut into thin strips (optional)
  Baked tortilla chips

In a medium bowl stir together lime juice and plum or peach jam until smooth. Stir in peach, strawberries, pineapple, plums, red onion, finely chopped jalapeño pepper, and cloves. Cover and chill up to 2 hours to blend flavors.

If desired, garnish with jalapeño pepper strips. Serve with baked tortilla chips. Makes 8 servings.

Nutrition information per serving: 114 calories, 2 g protein, 21 g carbohydrate, 2 g fat (0 g saturated), 0 mg cholesterol, 120 mg sodium.

Apples with Cinnamon-Cider Dip

Once cut, the apple slices brown quickly. Sprinkle with lemon or orange juice mixed with a little water, or treat them with an ascorbic acid color keeper.

2 tablespoons cornstarch
1 tablespoon brown sugar
1¼ cups apple cider
3 tablespoons honey
2 teaspoons lemon juice
½ teaspoon ground cinnamon
⅛ teaspoon salt (optional)
  Dash ground cloves
  Dash ground allspice
1 tablespoon butter or margarine
4 apples, cored and sliced

For dip, in a medium saucepan combine cornstarch and brown sugar. Stir in apple cider, honey, lemon juice, cinnamon, salt (if desired), cloves, and allspice. Cook and stir until thickened and bubbly. Cook and stir for 2 minutes more. Remove from heat.

Add butter or margarine, stirring until melted. Serve dip warm with sliced apples. Makes 4 to 6 servings.

Nutrition information per serving: 221 calories, 0 g protein, 51 g carbohydrate, 3 g fat (2 g saturated), 8 mg cholesterol, 34 mg sodium.

Apples with Cinnamon-Cider Dip

Potted Pepper Dip

For an eye-catching presentation, use an assortment of colorful sweet peppers. If you want to make a lower-fat dip, use fat-free cream cheese and fat-free mayonnaise or salad dressing in place of the regular products.

2	tablespoons lemon juice
2	teaspoons olive oil or cooking oil
1	teaspoon sugar
¼	teaspoon salt
	Dash black pepper
1	small onion, cut up
4	large red, green, yellow, or orange sweet peppers, seeded and cut up*
1	8-ounce package cream cheese, softened
¼	cup mayonnaise or salad dressing
1	teaspoon prepared horseradish
	Few dashes bottled hot pepper sauce
2	or 3 red, yellow, and/or orange sweet peppers, tops removed and seeded
	Assorted vegetable dippers and/or breadsticks
	Fresh herbs (optional)

In a blender container or food processor bowl combine the lemon juice, oil, sugar, salt, and black pepper. Add the onion and about one-third of the cut-up sweet peppers.

Cover and blend or process until smooth. Add the remaining cut-up sweet peppers. Cover and blend or process until smooth. Transfer the mixture to a medium bowl. Cover and let stand at room temperature at least 2 hours.

Place pureed vegetable mixture in a sieve and press gently to drain off excess liquid. In a medium bowl combine cream cheese, mayonnaise or salad dressing, horseradish, and hot pepper sauce. Stir in the pureed vegetable mixture. Cover and chill for 2 to 3 hours.

Spoon into the whole sweet pepper shells. Place filled peppers in the center of a serving platter; surround with vegetable dippers and/or breadsticks. If desired, garnish with fresh herbs. Makes about 2 cups.

*Note: To avoid getting tough pepper skins in the dip, cook seeded, quartered sweet peppers in boiling water for a few seconds. When cool enough to handle, peel off skins with a small knife and cut peppers into pieces.

Nutrition information per tablespoon dip: 46 calories, 1 g protein, 2 g carbohydrate, 4 g fat (2 g saturated), 9 mg cholesterol, 50 mg sodium.

Creamy Onion Dip

We pepped up this version of a popular dip with a little crumbled blue cheese.

1½ cups dairy sour cream
2 tablespoons dry onion soup mix
½ cup crumbed blue cheese (2 ounces)
   Snipped parsley (optional)
   Assorted vegetable dippers (such as carrot, zucchini, jicama, or red sweet pepper strips, and/or broccoli or cauliflower flowerets)

In a medium mixing bowl stir together the sour cream and dry onion soup mix. Stir in blue cheese. Cover and chill up to 48 hours.

If desired, sprinkle with snipped parsley. Serve with vegetable dippers. Makes about 1¾ cups.

Nutrition information per tablespoon dip: 37 calories, 1 g protein, 1 g carbohydrate, 3 g fat (2 g saturated), 7 mg cholesterol, 103 mg sodium.

Monterey Jack Fondue

Monterey Jack cheese could be called the American mozzarella. Long known in California, it became available across the nation in the late '60s. It's great shredded over Mexican foods, such as enchiladas, or used in a grilled cheese sandwich.

3 tablespoons margarine or butter
3 tablespoons all-purpose flour
1 teaspoon dried minced onion
⅛ teaspoon garlic powder
⅛ teaspoon ground red pepper
1 5-ounce can (⅔ cup) evaporated milk
½ cup chicken broth
1¼ cups shredded Monterey Jack cheese (5 ounces)
   French bread cubes

In a small saucepan melt margarine or butter. Stir in flour, dried minced onion, garlic powder, and red pepper. Stir in milk and chicken broth all at once.

Cook and stir until thickened and bubbly. Gradually add Monterey Jack cheese, stirring until cheese is melted. Transfer to a fondue pot; place over fondue burner.

Serve the fondue with bread cubes. (Add additional chicken broth, as necessary, for desired consistency.) Makes 6 servings.

Nutrition information per serving: 249 calories, 9 g protein, 18 g carbohydrate, 16 g fat (7 g saturated), 28 mg cholesterol, 418 mg sodium.

Deviled Peanuts

These spicy peanuts or pumpkin seeds make a perfect snack to serve with a before-dinner drink such as sparkling water, hot-style tomato juice, or Mexican beer.

2	tablespoons margarine or butter
1	tablespoon lime juice or lemon juice
1	teaspoon ground cumin
1	teaspoon black pepper
½	to 1 teaspoon ground red pepper
¼	teaspoon salt
3	cups raw peanuts or shelled raw pumpkin seeds (1 pound)

In a saucepan combine margarine or butter, lime juice or lemon juice, cumin, black pepper, ground red pepper, and salt. Cook and stir until margarine is melted. Stir in the peanuts or shelled pumpkin seeds. Toss lightly to coat.

Spread the peanuts or pumpkin seeds in a 13x9x2-inch baking pan. Bake in a 350° oven for 15 to 20 minutes or until toasted, stirring occasionally. Cool before serving. Makes 24 servings.

Nutrition information per serving: 114 calories, 5 g protein, 3 g carbohydrate, 10 g fat (2 g saturated), 0 mg cholesterol, 38 mg sodium.

Curried Snack Mix

Do you crave salty, high-fat snacks, such as potato chips? Bake a batch of this snack mix and you'll save yourself about half the calories and more than half the fat of a similar serving of fat-laden chips.

3	plain rice cakes, broken into bite-size pieces
1	cup bite-size corn square cereal or oyster crackers
¾	cup pretzel sticks, halved (1 ounce)
1	tablespoon margarine or butter, melted
1	teaspoon Worcestershire sauce
½	to ¾ teaspoon curry powder

In a 13x9x2-inch baking pan stir together broken rice cakes, corn cereal or oyster crackers, and pretzels. In a custard cup stir together melted margarine or butter, Worcestershire sauce, and curry powder.

Drizzle curry mixture over cereal mixture. Toss gently to coat. Bake in a 300° oven for 20 minutes, stirring twice. Cool before serving. Store leftovers in a tightly covered container. Makes 6 to 8 servings.

Nutrition information per serving: 76 calories, 1 g protein, 12 g carbohydrate, 2 g fat (1 g saturated), 0 mg cholesterol, 175 mg sodium.

Curried Snack Mix

Sugar and Spice Popcorn

Why eat plain popcorn when you can enjoy this version spiced with cinnamon, nutmeg, and ginger?

Nonstick spray coating
6 cups popped popcorn (using no oil)
2 tablespoons sugar
2 teaspoons water
¼ teaspoon ground cinnamon
⅛ teaspoon ground nutmeg
⅛ teaspoon ground ginger

Spray a 13x9x2-inch baking pan with nonstick coating. Place the popcorn in the pan.

In a small bowl stir together sugar, water, cinnamon, nutmeg, and ginger. Drizzle the spice mixture over popcorn. Toss gently to coat. Bake in a 350° oven for 15 minutes, stirring once or twice.

Transfer the hot popcorn to a large piece of foil. Cool completely. Store leftovers in a tightly covered container. Makes 8 servings.

Nutrition information per serving: 32 calories, 1 g protein, 7 g carbohydrate, 0 g fat (0 g saturated), 0 mg cholesterol, 0 mg sodium.

Nachos de Mer

If the Scandinavians had invented nachos, they might taste something like this. Reminiscent of the northlanders' famed open-faced sandwiches, toasted pita wedges are topped with a delicate seafood salad.

Toasted Pita Wedges
1 cup finely chopped, seeded plum tomatoes
⅓ cup finely chopped red or green sweet pepper
1½ cups chopped cooked shrimp or crabmeat
2 tablespoons mayonnaise or salad dressing
1 tablespoon finely chopped green onion
2 teaspoons Dijon-style mustard
1½ teaspoons snipped fresh dill
⅛ teaspoon salt
1½ cups shredded Havarti or Swiss cheese (6 ounces)

Prepare Toasted Pita Wedges. Set aside. In a small bowl combine tomatoes and sweet pepper. In a medium bowl combine shrimp or crabmeat, mayonnaise or salad dressing, green onion, mustard, dill, and salt. Stir in shredded cheese. If desired, cover and chill both mixtures up to 4 hours.

Place the pita wedges on 2 large baking sheets. Top with shrimp mixture. Bake in a 350° oven for 5 to 6 minutes or until cheese starts to melt. Top with tomato mixture. Serve warm. Makes 18 servings.

Toasted Pita Wedges: Split 3 *pita bread rounds* in half horizontally. Cut each circle into 6 wedges. Place the wedges in a single layer on 2 large baking sheets. Bake in a 350° oven for 8 to 10 minutes or until wedges just start to brown. If desired, seal cooled wedges in a plastic bag and store overnight at room temperature. Makes 36 wedges.

Nutrition information per serving: 91 calories, 6 g protein, 7 g carbohydrate, 4 g fat (2 g saturated), 34 mg cholesterol, 145 mg sodium.

HELP YOURSELF TO HAVARTI

When you're looking for an appetizer cheese to serve with wine or to use in recipes such as Nachos de Mer (above), Havarti (ha-VART-ee) is hard to beat. This cream-colored cheese has a porous texture with small irregular holes and varies in flavor from mild to pungent. Besides making great appetizers, Havarti also is delicious in sandwiches or as a dessert with fruit.

Ratatouille Pizza

A ready-made Italian bread shell makes pizza preparation ever so easy. This garden-fresh version takes four different vegetables, arranges them on top of a tongue-tingling tomato sauce, and sprinkles the entire concoction with feta and mozzarella cheeses.

---

1 small eggplant (12 ounces)
2 tablespoons olive oil or cooking oil
½ cup chopped onion
2 cloves garlic, minced
4 medium tomatoes, peeled, seeded, and chopped (about 2⅔ cups)
1 tablespoon snipped fresh oregano or thyme, or 1 teaspoon dried oregano or thyme, crushed
½ teaspoon sugar
¼ teaspoon salt
⅛ teaspoon pepper
1 12-inch Italian bread shell (Boboli)
2 medium red and/or yellow tomatoes, halved lengthwise and thinly sliced
1 small zucchini, thinly sliced
1 small yellow summer squash, thinly sliced
⅓ cup crumbled feta cheese
2 tablespoons sliced pitted ripe olives
½ cup shredded mozzarella cheese (2 ounces)
   Small fresh oregano or thyme leaves (optional)

Chop enough of the eggplant to make 1 cup. Halve the remaining eggplant lengthwise and thinly slice.

In a medium skillet heat 1 tablespoon of the oil. Add onion and garlic and cook until onion is tender. Stir in chopped eggplant, chopped tomatoes, snipped fresh or dried oregano or thyme, sugar, salt, and pepper. Cook, uncovered, over medium-low heat about 15 minutes or until liquid is evaporated and mixture is of spreading consistency, stirring occasionally during cooking. Remove from heat.

Place the bread shell on a lightly greased baking sheet. Spread the warm tomato mixture over bread shell. Arrange the eggplant and tomato slices around the outside edge of the bread shell. Arrange zucchini and yellow squash slices in the center. Brush vegetables with the remaining oil. Sprinkle with feta cheese and olives. Top with mozzarella cheese.

Bake in a 400° oven for 12 to 15 minutes or until the vegetables are warm and cheese is melted. Transfer to a serving platter. If desired, garnish with fresh oregano or thyme leaves. Cut into wedges. Makes 12 servings.

Nutrition information per serving: 180 calories, 8 g protein, 23 g carbohydrate, 7 g fat (2 g saturated), 11 mg cholesterol, 366 mg sodium.

Fruited Cheese Spirals

Finger food gets a fresh new look! Dried fruit adds jewel tones to these clever spirals filled with prosciutto, cream cheese, and the cinnamon-pepper flavor of fresh basil.

½ cup orange juice or apple juice
1 cup dried fruit (such as cranberries, snipped tart or sweet cherries, and/or snipped apricots)
1 8-ounce tub cream cheese
½ cup dairy sour cream or plain yogurt
¼ cup fresh basil leaves, finely snipped
2 14- to 15-inch soft cracker bread rounds or four 7- to 8-inch flour tortillas
4 very thin slices prosciutto or fully cooked ham
Fresh basil leaves (optional)
Orange slices (optional)

In a small saucepan bring the orange juice or apple juice to boiling. Stir in dried fruit; remove from heat. Cover and let stand about 15 minutes or until fruit is softened. Drain. Meanwhile, in a medium mixing bowl stir together cream cheese, sour cream or yogurt, and the ¼ cup finely snipped basil.

Spread cream cheese mixture evenly over one side of each cracker bread or tortilla. Sprinkle each with the softened fruit. Place some of the prosciutto or ham near an edge of each round. Starting from the edge closest to meat, tightly roll up. Wrap each roll in plastic wrap and chill for 4 to 24 hours.

To serve, cut each roll into 1-inch slices. If desired, garnish with additional basil leaves and orange slices. Makes about 24 servings.

Nutrition information per serving: 115 calories, 3 g protein, 14 g carbohydrate, 6 g fat (2 g saturated), 12 mg cholesterol, 142 mg sodium.

*A*PPETIZER PARTY HINTS

When you plan an appetizer party, imagine how foods will look and taste together. Balance rich, highly flavored foods with simple, fresh ones. Plan one or two hot appetizers that can be made ahead and heated just before serving. Also select several chilled appetizers that can be prepared early and served without last-minute attention. If you serve buffet style, choose foods that guests can pick up easily. Too many choices that must be spooned out, sliced, or spread may cause people to bunch around the buffet table.

Jamaican Shrimp

Jamaican cooks usually use Scotch bonnet peppers instead of jalapeño peppers in their spicy dishes. Scotch bonnets, one of the hottest of the chile peppers, add fire to this recipe. Use them if they're available and you like your shrimp hot, hot, hot.

2 pounds fresh or frozen large shrimp in shells
¼ cup salad oil
3 tablespoons white wine vinegar
2 tablespoons lime juice
1 jalapeño pepper, seeded and finely chopped
1 tablespoon honey
2 teaspoons Jamaican Jerk Seasoning
Leaf lettuce (optional)
1 medium mango, peeled, pitted, sliced, and halved crosswise
1 small lime, halved lengthwise and sliced
1 small red onion, quartered and thinly sliced

Rinse shrimp. In a large saucepan cook the fresh or frozen shrimp in boiling, lightly salted water for 1 to 3 minutes or until shrimp turn pink. Drain immediately and cool. Peel and devein shrimp, leaving tails intact. Place shrimp in a plastic bag and set the bag into a shallow dish. (At this point, you can seal the bag and chill up to 24 hours.)

For marinade, in a screw-top jar combine oil, white wine vinegar, lime juice, jalapeño pepper, honey, and Jamaican Jerk Seasoning. Cover and shake well. Pour over the shrimp; seal bag. Marinate in the refrigerator for 1 hour, turning bag occasionally.

Drain shrimp, reserving marinade. If desired, line a large platter with lettuce. Arrange the shrimp, mango, lime, and red onion on top of lettuce. Drizzle with the marinade. Makes 10 to 12 servings.

Jamaican Jerk Seasoning: In a small mixing bowl combine 2 teaspoons *onion powder*, 1 teaspoon *sugar*, 1 teaspoon *salt*, 1 teaspoon ground *thyme*, ½ teaspoon ground *allspice*, ¼ teaspoon ground *cinnamon*, and ¼ teaspoon ground *red pepper*.

Nutrition information per serving: 128 calories, 11 g protein, 7 g carbohydrate, 6 g fat (1 g saturated), 105 mg cholesterol, 174 mg sodium.

Frosty Fruit Smoothie

Here's a kid-pleasing snack that's especially rich in vitamin C.

1 medium banana, peeled and cut into chunks 1 cup orange, pineapple, grape, or apple juice or low-calorie cranberry juice, chilled ½ cup fat-free milk 1 teaspoon vanilla 3 ice cubes	In a blender container combine the banana chunks, chilled fruit juice, milk, vanilla, and ice cubes. Cover and blend until frothy. Pour mixture into glasses. Serve immediately. Makes 2 (10-ounce) servings. *Nutrition information per serving: 137 calories, 4 g protein, 30 g carbohydrate, 1 g fat (0 g saturated), 1 mg cholesterol, 34 mg sodium.*

Apple Sunrise

Make ice cubes from apple or cranberry juice to float in a glass of this refreshing drink.

1 cup apple juice or apple cider, chilled 1 cup low-calorie cranberry juice, chilled ½ cup chilled club soda Ice cubes 2 orange slices (optional)	In a 1-quart measuring cup stir together apple juice or cider, cranberry juice, and club soda. Fill tall glasses with ice cubes. Pour the apple juice mixture over ice. If desired, cut a slit in each orange slice and twist one over the rim of each glass. Makes 2 (10-ounce) servings. *Nutrition information per serving: 85 calories, 0 g protein, 21 g carbohydrate, 0 g fat (0 g saturated), 0 mg cholesterol, 26 mg sodium.*

Iced Espresso

Orange Yogurt Drink

Yogurt, fat-free milk, and fat-free sour cream make this beverage taste positively dreamy.

2½ cups fat-free milk
 2 8-ounce cartons vanilla, lemon, or
     orange low-fat yogurt
 ½ cup fat-free or light dairy sour cream
 ¼ cup frozen orange or apple juice
     concentrate, thawed

In a pitcher combine milk, yogurt, sour cream, and orange or apple juice concentrate. Beat with a wire whisk or rotary beater until smooth.

Serve immediately or chill. Store leftovers in the refrigerator. Makes 8 (5-ounce) servings.

Nutrition information per serving: 116 calories, 7 g protein, 19 g carbohydrate, 1 g fat (1 g saturated), 5 mg cholesterol, 90 mg sodium.

Iced Espresso

Besides being a refreshing between-meal pick-me-up, this frosty coffee drink is wonderful after a light lunch or dinner in place of dessert.

 ½ cup ground espresso coffee or
     French roast coffee
 1 teaspoon finely shredded orange
     peel
 4 cups water
1½ cups fat-free milk
 3 tablespoons sugar
     Ice cubes
     Orange peel strips (optional)
 1 teaspoon grated semisweet chocolate
     (optional)

Prepare coffee with shredded orange peel and water in a drip coffeemaker or percolator according to the manufacturer's directions. Pour into a heatproof pitcher; stir in milk and sugar. Chill until serving time.

To serve, fill 6 glasses with ice cubes. Pour the coffee mixture over the ice. If desired, garnish each serving with an orange peel strip and grated chocolate. Makes 6 (6-ounce) servings.

Nutrition information per serving: 54 calories, 2 g protein, 11 g carbohydrate, 0 g fat (0 g saturated), 1 mg cholesterol, 35 mg sodium.

SPICY STEAK & RANCH SALAD
(recipe, page 26)

Salads,
SOUPS & STEWS

Contents

Taco Salad

Although a tomatillo (tohm ah TEE oh) looks like a small green tomato, its flavor is a combination of lemon, apple, and herbs. Look for canned tomatillos in the Mexican foods section of your supermarket.

Tortilla Cups
Tomatillo Guacamole
8 ounces lean ground beef
3 cloves garlic, minced
1 15-ounce can dark red kidney beans, rinsed and drained
1 8-ounce jar taco sauce
¾ cup frozen whole kernel corn
1 tablespoon chili powder
8 cups torn leaf lettuce or iceberg lettuce
2 medium tomatoes, chopped
1 large green sweet pepper, chopped
¾ cup shredded sharp cheddar cheese (3 ounces)
4 green onions, thinly sliced

Prepare Tortilla Cups; set aside. Prepare Tomatillo Guacamole; chill.

In a medium skillet cook ground beef and garlic until beef is brown. Drain off fat. Stir in beans, taco sauce, corn, and chili powder. Bring to boiling; reduce heat. Cover and simmer for 10 minutes.

In large bowl combine lettuce, tomatoes, green pepper, cheese, and green onions. Divide the lettuce mixture among the Tortilla Cups. Top each with some of the beef mixture and the Tomatillo Guacamole. Makes 6 servings.

Tortilla Cups: Lightly brush six 9- or 10-inch *flour tortillas* with a small amount of *water* or spray *nonstick spray coating* onto 1 side of each tortilla. Spray nonstick coating into 6 small oven-safe bowls or 16-ounce individual casseroles. Press tortillas, coated sides up, into bowls or casseroles. Place a ball of foil into each tortilla cup. Bake in a 350° oven for 15 to 20 minutes or until light brown. Remove foil; cool. Remove Tortilla Cups from bowls. Serve immediately or store in an airtight container for up to 5 days.

Tomatillo Guacamole: Rinse, drain, and finely chop 4 canned *tomatillos* (about ⅓ cup). In a small mixing bowl combine tomatillos; ½ of a small seeded, peeled, and chopped *avocado* (about ½ cup); 2 tablespoons chopped canned *green chile peppers,* drained; and ⅛ teaspoon *garlic salt.* Cover and chill for up to 24 hours. Makes about ¾ cup.

Nutrition information per serving: 398 calories, 22 g protein, 49 g carbohydrate, 17 g fat (6 g saturated), 38 mg cholesterol, 801 mg sodium.

Spicy Steak & Ranch Salad

Steak and onions as you've never seen them before! Sirloin is perked up by Cajun seasoning before slicing, then arranged on tossed greens and topped with a scattering of crispy French-fried onions. This new version of the classic combo has the makings of an instant favorite.

½ cup French-fried onions
1 tablespoon Cajun seasoning
1 tablespoon lime juice
1 clove garlic, minced
1 pound boneless beef top sirloin steak, cut 1 inch thick
  Salt (optional)
1 10-ounce package European-style salad greens (iceberg lettuce, romaine, radicchio, escarole, and endive)
2 carrots, peeled into thin strips or cut into thin bite-size strips
½ cup thinly sliced radishes
½ cup bottled fat-free ranch salad dressing

In a large nonstick skillet cook French-fried onions over medium-high heat about 2 minutes or until browned, stirring occasionally. Set aside.

Meanwhile, combine Cajun seasoning, lime juice, and garlic; rub over both sides of steak. In the same skillet cook steak over medium heat to desired doneness, turning once. (Allow 6 to 8 minutes for medium rare or 9 to 12 minutes for medium.) Remove skillet from heat; let stand for 10 minutes. Cut steak into thin bite-size slices. If desired, season with salt.

In a large bowl toss together the salad greens, carrots, and radishes. Divide among 4 salad bowls or plates. Arrange steak strips over greens mixture. Drizzle dressing over salads. Sprinkle with onions. Makes 4 servings.

Nutrition information per serving: 310 calories, 28 g protein, 16 g carbohydrate, 13 g fat (4 g saturated fat), 76 mg cholesterol, 557 mg sodium.

Pacific Rim Grilled Pork Salad

This dazzling salad blends grilled pork with ingredients from the cuisines of the eastern rim of the Pacific Ocean—soy sauce, ginger, hoisin sauce, rice wine vinegar, sesame oil, and enoki mushrooms.

⅓ cup water
¼ cup dry sherry
¼ cup soy sauce
4 teaspoons grated gingerroot
3 cloves garlic, minced
1 1½-pound boneless pork loin roast, cut into ½-inch-thick slices
¼ cup hoisin sauce
2 tablespoons brown sugar
2 tablespoons salad oil
2 tablespoons rice wine vinegar or white wine vinegar
1 tablespoon toasted sesame oil
12 cups torn spinach
6 thin red onion slices, separated into rings
1 tablespoon sesame seed, toasted (optional)
1 pound plums, pitted and sliced (3 cups)
Enoki mushrooms (optional)

For marinade, in a small mixing bowl combine water, sherry, soy sauce, gingerroot, and garlic. Reserve 2 tablespoons of the marinade for the dressing. Place meat in a plastic bag set in a large bowl. Pour remaining marinade over meat. Close bag. Marinate in the refrigerator for 1 hour.

Drain meat; discard marinade. Grill meat on uncovered grill directly over medium-hot coals for 10 to 12 minutes or until slightly pink in center, turning once.

Meanwhile, for dressing, in a saucepan combine the reserved marinade, hoisin sauce, brown sugar, salad oil, and rice wine vinegar or white wine vinegar. Bring to boiling. Stir in sesame oil. Remove from heat.

Thinly slice meat into bite-size strips. In a large salad bowl combine meat, spinach, onion slices, and, if desired, sesame seed. Pour hot dressing over meat mixture. Toss gently to coat.

Serve on salad plates with plum slices. If desired, top with enoki mushrooms. Makes 6 servings.

Nutrition information per serving: 310 calories, 21 g protein, 22 g carbohydrate, 16 g fat (4 g saturated), 51 mg cholesterol, 1,159 mg sodium.

Peppered Pork & Apricot Salad

Dazzle guests with a main-dish salad whose vibrant colors—bright green, apricot, and black and cream—make a statement on the serving plates. Use quick-cooking pork tenderloin, then slice it into appealing medallions.

12 ounces pork tenderloin
1 teaspoon coarsely ground pepper
1 6-ounce package long-grain and wild rice mix
½ cup snipped dried apricots
¼ cup fat-free Italian salad dressing
2 green onions, thinly sliced
2 tablespoons frozen orange juice concentrate, thawed
½ cup frozen peas
   Fresh apricots, pitted and sliced (optional)

Trim fat from meat. Place meat on a rack in a shallow roasting pan. Sprinkle the meat with pepper. Insert a meat thermometer into the center of meat. Roast, uncovered, in a 425° oven for 25 to 35 minutes or until the meat thermomter registers 155°. Remove from oven and cover with foil. Let stand for 10 minutes.

Meanwhile, prepare rice mix according to package directions, adding the dried apricots during the last 5 minutes of cooking. Spread mixture in a shallow baking pan and cool for 20 minutes.

For dressing, in a small bowl combine salad dressing, green onions, and orange juice concentrate. In a large bowl combine rice mixture and peas. Drizzle with dressing. Toss gently to coat. Spoon rice mixture onto salad plates. Cut meat crosswise into thin slices; arrange meat on rice mixture. If desired, garnish with fresh apricots. Makes 4 servings.

Nutrition information per serving: 356 calories, 25 g protein, 50 g carbohydrate, 6 g fat (2 g saturated), 61 mg cholesterol, 1,056 mg sodium.

SNIPPING APRICOTS MADE EASY

To snip dried apricots quickly and easily, place apricot halves in a 1-cup glass measure and use kitchen shears or scissors to snip the fruit. Dipping the shears in cold water between snips will keep the apricot pieces from sticking to the shears.

Greek Salad with Herb Vinaigrette

No leftover lamb around? Broil some lamb chops to medium-rare. Then, chill the chops completely before slicing them into thin strips.

3 cups torn curly endive or romaine

1½ cups torn spinach or iceberg lettuce

6 ounces cooked lean lamb or beef, cut into bite-size strips

1 medium tomato, chopped

½ small cucumber, thinly sliced

6 radishes, sliced

2 tablespoons sliced pitted ripe olives

½ cup crumbled feta cheese (2 ounces)

2 green onions, thinly sliced

½ cup Herb Vinaigrette

3 anchovy fillets, drained, rinsed, and patted dry (optional)

Toss together curly endive or romaine and spinach or lettuce. Divide greens among 3 salad plates.

Arrange meat strips, chopped tomato, sliced cucumber, sliced radishes, and olives on greens. Sprinkle with feta cheese and green onions. Shake Herb Vinaigrette well. Drizzle over salads. If desired, top with anchovy fillets. Makes 3 servings.

Herb Vinaigrette: In a screw-top jar combine ½ cup *salad oil;* ⅓ cup *white wine vinegar* or *vinegar;* 1 tablespoon *sugar;* 2 teaspoons snipped *fresh* or ½ teaspoon crushed *dried thyme, oregano,* or *basil;* ½ teaspoon *paprika;* ¼ teaspoon *dry mustard;* and ⅛ teaspoon *pepper.* Cover and shake well. Store dressing in the refrigerator for up to 2 weeks. Shake well before using. Makes about ¾ cup.

Nutrition information per serving: 431 calories, 20 g protein, 11 g carbohydrate, 35 g fat (8 g saturated), 69 mg cholesterol, 325 mg sodium.

CURLY ENDIVE CUES

Also known as chicory, curly endive has crisp, frilly, narrow dark green leaves and a prickly texture. Look for heads with crisp, fresh leaves and no discoloration. Store the endive tightly wrapped in the refrigerator for up to 3 days. To use, rinse well in cold water and pat dry with paper towels.

Garlic-Ginger Chicken Strip Salad

If you're watching your sodium, switch to reduced-sodium soy sauce.

4   small skinless, boneless chicken
      breast halves (about 12 ounces
      total)
¼   cup soy sauce
¼   cup dry sherry
1   tablespoon snipped fresh basil or
      1 teaspoon dried basil, crushed
1   tablespoon honey
2   teaspoons grated gingerroot
½   teaspoon crushed red pepper
½   teaspoon black pepper
¼   teaspoon five-spice powder
4   cloves garlic, minced
2   cups broccoli flowerets
5   cups torn mixed greens
1   cup enoki mushrooms or sliced fresh
      mushrooms
1   medium red sweet pepper, cut into
      ¾-inch pieces (1 cup)
1   cup coarsely chopped red cabbage
      Oriental Salad Dressing
      Leaf lettuce

Rinse chicken; pat dry. Cut breast halves into bite-size strips. For marinade, in a medium mixing bowl combine soy sauce, sherry, basil, honey, gingerroot, crushed red pepper, black pepper, five-spice powder, and garlic. Add chicken strips; stir to coat. Cover and marinate in the refrigerator for 4 to 24 hours.

Drain chicken strips, reserving marinade. Place chicken on unheated rack of a broiler pan. Broil 4 to 5 inches from heat about 5 minutes or until light brown, brushing once with reserved marinade. Turn and brush again. Broil 3 to 5 minutes more or until chicken is tender and no longer pink. Discard remaining marinade.

Meanwhile, in a covered medium saucepan cook the broccoli in a small amount of boiling water for 1 minute. Drain well and chill.

In a large mixing bowl toss together torn mixed greens, mushrooms, red sweet pepper, red cabbage, and cooked broccoli. Shake Oriental Salad Dressing well. Pour about ½ cup of the dressing over greens mixture; toss lightly to coat. Line 4 salad plates with leaf lettuce. Divide greens mixture among salad plates. Top with chicken strips. Drizzle remaining dressing over chicken. Makes 4 servings.

Oriental Salad Dressing: In a screw-top jar combine ⅓ cup unsweetened *pineapple juice,* ¼ cup *rice vinegar* or *white vinegar,* 1 tablespoon *soy sauce,* 2 teaspoons *sugar,* 1½ teaspoons toasted *sesame oil,* and ¼ teaspoon *black pepper.* Cover and shake well. Makes ⅔ cup.

Nutrition information per serving: 235 calories, 21 g protein, 26 g carbohydrate, 5 g fat (1 g saturated), 45 mg cholesterol, 1,368 mg sodium.

Salmon-Pasta Salad

Fold the salmon gently into the pasta mixture so it stays in nice big chunks.

1	cup packaged dried corkscrew macaroni or medium shell macaroni
1½	cups broccoli flowerets
4	ounces Gruyère or Swiss cheese, cut into thin, bite-size strips
¼	cup sliced radishes
⅔	cup mayonnaise or salad dressing
1	tablespoon snipped fresh basil or 1 teaspoon dried basil, crushed
2	teaspoons white wine Worcestershire sauce
⅛	teaspoon garlic salt
1	to 2 tablespoons milk
1	15½-ounce can salmon, chilled
	Leaf lettuce
	Pineapple sage flowers (optional)

In a large saucepan cook pasta in boiling salted water for 9 minutes. Add broccoli; return to boiling. Cook about 4 minutes more or until pasta and broccoli are tender. Drain the pasta and broccoli; rinse with cold water. Drain again.

In a large mixing bowl combine cooked pasta-broccoli mixture, Gruyère or Swiss cheese, and radishes.

For dressing, in a small mixing bowl stir together the mayonnaise or salad dressing, basil, white wine Worcestershire sauce, and garlic salt. Stir in enough of the milk to make desired consistency. Pour dressing over pasta mixture. Toss lightly to mix. Cover and chill for 4 to 24 hours.

Before serving, if necessary, stir a little additional milk into the pasta mixture to moisten. Drain and flake salmon, discarding skin and bones. Fold salmon into salad mixture.

Line 4 salad plates with leaf lettuce. Divide the salmon mixture among plates. If desired, garnish with pineapple sage flowers. Makes 4 servings.

Nutrition information per serving: 641 calories, 36 g protein, 19 g carbohydrate, 47 g fat (12 g saturated), 101 mg cholesterol, 999 mg sodium.

Seafood Louis Salad

Using a blend of low-fat cottage cheese and fat-free milk, instead of the traditional mayonnaise and whipping cream, eliminates about 30 grams of fat and makes this classic salad guilt-free for fat-watchers.

1 6-ounce package frozen, peeled, cooked shrimp
½ cup low-fat cottage cheese
2 tablespoons fat-free milk
1 tablespoon tomato paste
2 tablespoons chopped red sweet pepper or diced pimiento
1 green onion, thinly sliced
⅛ teaspoon salt
⅛ teaspoon black pepper
6 cups torn romaine
1 cup shredded red cabbage
1 medium carrot, shredded (½ cup)
1 6-ounce can crabmeat, drained, flaked, and cartilage removed
2 tomatoes, cut into thin wedges
Carrot curls (optional)

Thaw shrimp. For dressing, in a blender container or food processor bowl combine cottage cheese, milk, and tomato paste. Cover and blend or process until smooth. Transfer mixture to a small bowl. Stir in red pepper or pimiento, green onion, salt, black pepper, and enough additional fat-free milk to make dressing of desired consistency. Cover and chill till serving time.

In a large bowl toss together romaine, red cabbage, and shredded carrot. Divide among salad plates. Arrange shrimp, crabmeat, and tomatoes on each plate. Drizzle with dressing. If desired, garnish with carrot curls. Pass any remaining dressing. Makes 3 servings.

Nutrition information per serving: 207 calories, 31 g protein, 14 g carbohydrate, 3 g fat (1 g saturated), 171 mg cholesterol, 729 mg sodium.

Texas-Style Bowls of Red

Texans have a high tolerance for hot and spicy foods, so if you're not from the Lone Star State, taste this extra-hot, authentic chili at your own risk!

20 small dried hot chile peppers or
    2 tablespoons crushed red pepper
 2 dried ancho peppers or
    2 tablespoons chili powder
12 ounces beef round steak
12 ounces lean boneless pork
 2 tablespoons cooking oil
 1 cup chopped onion
 1 tablespoon ground cumin
 3 cloves garlic, minced
 ½ teaspoon paprika
 ¼ teaspoon black pepper
 1 14½-ounce can beef broth
 1 12-ounce can beer
 3 cups hot cooked pinto beans and/or
    hot cooked rice
    Sliced jalapeño peppers (optional)

Crush hot chile peppers (if using). Remove stems and seeds from ancho peppers (if using); cut into 1-inch pieces. Place hot peppers and ancho peppers in a blender container or food processor bowl. Cover and blend or process until ground. Let pepper dust settle before opening blender or food processor. (If using crushed red pepper and chili powder, stir them together.) Set aside.

Trim fat from meat. Cut into ½-inch cubes. In a large saucepan or Dutch oven cook half of the meat in hot oil until brown. Remove meat and set aside. Add the remaining meat, onion, cumin, garlic, paprika, black pepper, and ground hot pepper or chili powder mixture. Cook until meat is brown. Return all meat to saucepan. Add beef broth and beer.

Bring to boiling; reduce heat. Cover and simmer for 45 minutes. Uncover and simmer about 30 minutes more or until meat is tender and broth mixture is desired consistency, stirring occasionally. Serve with hot cooked pinto beans and/or rice. If desired, garnish with jalapeño peppers. Makes 6 servings.

Nutrition information per serving: 340 calories, 26 g protein, 34 g carbohydrate, 10 g fat (2 g saturated), 44 mg cholesterol, 445 mg sodium.

Tuscan Sausage and Bean Soup

By using the crockery cooker method, you can have a dynamite Italian-style dinner ready when you step in the door, even if you were on the go all day.

1¼ cups dry Great Northern beans
1¾ cups beef broth
½ cup chopped onion
1 clove garlic, minced
½ teaspoon dried Italian seasoning, crushed
12 ounces uncooked Italian sausage links, cut into ½-inch slices
1 medium yellow summer squash or zucchini, sliced (2 cups)
1 14½-ounce can Italian-style tomatoes, cut up
⅓ cup dry red wine or water
½ of a 10-ounce package frozen chopped spinach, thawed and well drained
Grated Parmesan cheese (optional)

Rinse beans. In a large saucepan or Dutch oven combine beans and 4 cups cold water. Bring to boiling; reduce heat. Simmer, uncovered, for 2 minutes. Remove from heat. Cover and let stand for 1 hour. (Or, place beans in water in pan. Cover and soak beans overnight.) Drain and rinse beans.

In the same pan combine beans, 4 cups fresh water, beef broth, onion, garlic, and Italian seasoning. Bring to boiling; reduce heat. Cover and simmer about 2 hours or until beans are tender.

Meanwhile, in a medium skillet cook sliced Italian sausage until brown. Drain well on paper towels. Add cooked sausage, yellow squash or zucchini, undrained tomatoes, and red wine or water to bean mixture. Bring to boiling; reduce heat. Cover and simmer about 5 minutes more or until squash is tender.

Stir in spinach. Heat through. If desired, sprinkle each serving with Parmesan cheese. Makes 4 or 5 servings.

Crockery-Cooker Directions: Rinse beans. In a large saucepan combine beans and 4 cups cold water. Simmer, uncovered, for 10 minutes; drain. Prepare sausage as above. In a 3½- to 4-quart crockery cooker combine beans, 4 cups fresh water, beef broth, onion, garlic, Italian seasoning, cooked sausage, squash, undrained tomatoes, and red wine or water. Cover and cook on low heat setting for 11 to 12 hours or until beans are tender. Just before serving, stir spinach into soup. If desired, sprinkle each serving with cheese.

Nutrition information per serving: 563 calories, 36 g protein, 63 g carbohydrate, 19 g fat (6 g saturated), 49 mg cholesterol, 1,155 mg sodium.

Mexican Chicken-Tortilla Soup

This soup features cilantro, a fresh herb that looks like a flattened parsley leaf but has a pungent, almost musty odor and taste that gives a distinctive flavor to Mexican dishes.

2 whole small chicken breasts
(about 1¼ pounds total)
3½ cups chicken broth
½ cup chopped onion
1 clove garlic, minced
½ teaspoon ground cumin
1 tablespoon cooking oil
1 14½-ounce can tomatoes, cut up
1 8-ounce can tomato sauce
1 4-ounce can whole green chile
peppers, rinsed, seeded, and cut
into thin bite-size strips
¼ cup snipped cilantro or parsley
1 tablespoon snipped fresh oregano or
1 teaspoon dried oregano, crushed
6 6-inch corn tortillas
Cooking oil
1 cup shredded cheddar or Monterey
Jack cheese (4 ounces)

Rinse chicken. In a large saucepan or Dutch oven combine chicken and chicken broth. Bring to boiling; reduce heat. Cover and simmer about 15 minutes or until chicken is tender and no longer pink. Remove chicken. Set aside to cool. Skin, bone, and finely shred chicken. Set chicken aside. Discard skin and bones. Strain broth through a large sieve or colander lined with two layers of 100% cotton cheesecloth. Skim fat from broth and set broth aside.

In the same saucepan cook onion, garlic, and cumin in 1 tablespoon hot oil until onion is tender. Stir in strained broth, undrained tomatoes, tomato sauce, chile peppers, cilantro or parsley, and oregano. Bring to boiling; reduce heat. Cover and simmer for 20 minutes. Stir in shredded chicken. Heat through.

Meanwhile, cut tortillas in half, then cut crosswise into ½-inch-wide strips. In a heavy medium skillet heat ¼ inch oil. Cook strips in hot oil, half at a time, about 1 minute or until crisp and light brown. Remove with a slotted spoon; drain on paper towels.

Divide fried tortilla strips among soup bowls. Ladle soup over tortilla strips. Sprinkle each serving with shredded cheese. Serve immediately. Makes 4 servings.

Nutrition information per serving: 496 calories, 38 g protein, 33 g carbohydrate, 24 g fat (8 g saturated), 85 mg cholesterol, 1,658 mg sodium.

Cream of Chile-Chicken Soup

Ground red pepper and green chile peppers add a spiciness to this creamy soup. For an accompaniment, serve some cornbread or cornsticks with it.

8 ounces ground raw chicken or turkey
¼ cup chopped onion
2 cloves garlic, minced
2 cups milk
1 10¾-ounce can condensed cream of chicken soup
1 7-ounce can whole kernel corn with sweet peppers, drained
1 medium tomato, chopped (¾ cup)
1 4-ounce can diced green chile peppers, drained
2 tablespoons snipped cilantro or parsley
¼ teaspoon ground red pepper
1 cup shredded Monterey Jack cheese (4 ounces)

In a large saucepan or Dutch oven cook ground chicken or turkey, onion, and garlic until chicken or turkey is no longer pink and onion is tender. Drain fat, if necessary.

Stir in milk, cream of chicken soup, corn, chopped tomato, chile peppers, cilantro or parsley, and ground red pepper. Bring to boiling; reduce heat. Simmer, uncovered, for 5 minutes, stirring occasionally.

Add Monterey Jack cheese. Cook and stir until cheese is melted. Makes 4 servings.

Nutrition information per serving: 375 calories, 24 g protein, 29 g carbohydrate, 19 g fat (9 g saturated), 68 mg cholesterol, 1,481 mg sodium.

Broth Options

Many of the recipes in this chapter call for chicken, beef, or vegetable broth. If you're out of canned broth, you can use bouillon granules or cubes as a substitute. Just remember that 1 cup of canned broth is equivalent to 1 teaspoon of granules or 1 cube dissolved in 1 cup water. Look for these products with the soups at your supermarket.

Chunky Vegetable-Cod Soup

This fish soup will win your family's approval … hook, line, and sinker!

1	pound fresh or frozen skinless cod fillets or steaks
½	cup chopped red sweet pepper
¼	cup chopped onion
1	tablespoon margarine or butter
3½	cups vegetable broth or chicken broth
1	cup frozen cut green beans
1	cup coarsely chopped cabbage
½	cup sliced carrot
1	teaspoon snipped fresh basil
1	teaspoon snipped fresh thyme
½	teaspoon snipped fresh rosemary
¼	teaspoon black pepper
	Lemon wedges (optional)

Thaw fish, if frozen. Rinse fish. Cut into 1-inch pieces. In a large saucepan or Dutch oven cook red pepper and onion in margarine or butter until tender.

Stir in the broth, green beans, cabbage, carrot, basil, thyme, rosemary, and black pepper. Bring to boiling; reduce heat. Cover and simmer for 8 to 10 minutes or until vegetables are nearly tender.

Stir fish into broth mixture. Return to boiling; reduce heat. Cover and simmer about 5 minutes or until fish flakes easily with a fork, stirring once. If desired, serve with lemon wedges. Makes 4 servings.

Nutrition information per serving: 140 calories, 20 g protein, 9 g carbohydrate, 5 g fat (1 g saturated), 45 mg cholesterol, 922 mg sodium.

Manhattan Fish Chowder

Manhattan-style chowders are tomato-based and may contain other vegetables in place of the potatoes found in milk-based New England-style chowders.

12	ounces fresh or frozen fish fillets
1	24-ounce can vegetable juice
1	11-ounce can whole kernel corn with sweet peppers
½	cup sliced green onions
¼	cup chicken broth
1½	teaspoons snipped fresh thyme or ½ teaspoon dried thyme, crushed
1	teaspoon Worcestershire sauce
	Several dashes bottled hot pepper sauce

Thaw fish, if frozen. Rinse fish. Cut fish into ¾-inch pieces. In a large saucepan combine vegetable juice, corn, green onions, broth, thyme, Worcestershire sauce, and hot pepper sauce. Bring to boiling; reduce heat. Cover and simmer for 8 minutes.

Stir fish into juice mixture. Return to boiling; reduce heat. Cover and simmer for 3 to 5 minutes more or until fish flakes easily with a fork, stirring once. Makes 4 servings.

Nutrition information per serving: 164 calories, 16 g protein, 22 g carbohydrate, 1 g fat (0 g saturated), 34 mg cholesterol, 995 mg sodium.

Chunky Vegetable-Cod Soup

Minestrone

The countless versions of this classic Italian soup all have one thing in common—they're full of beans, pasta, and vegetables.

2   14½-ounce cans chicken broth or beef broth
1   14½-ounce can tomatoes, cut up
1   cup chopped onion
1   cup shredded cabbage
¾   cup tomato juice
½   cup chopped carrot
½   cup sliced celery
1   tablespoon snipped fresh basil or 1 teaspoon dried basil, crushed
¼   teaspoon garlic powder
1   15-ounce can white kidney (cannellini) beans or Great Northern beans, rinsed and drained
1   medium zucchini, sliced ¼ inch thick (1 cup)
½   of a 9-ounce package frozen Italian-style green beans
2   ounces packaged dried spaghetti or linguine, broken (about ½ cup)
2   tablespoons shaved or finely shredded Parmesan cheese

In a Dutch oven combine broth, undrained tomatoes, onion, cabbage, tomato juice, carrot, celery, basil, and garlic powder. Bring to boiling; reduce heat. Cover and simmer for 20 minutes.

Stir in white kidney or Great Northern beans, zucchini, green beans, and pasta. Return to boiling; reduce heat. Cover and simmer for 10 to 15 minutes more or until vegetables and pasta are tender.

Ladle into soup bowls. Sprinkle each serving with Parmesan cheese. Makes 4 servings.

Nutrition information per serving: 243 calories, 17 g protein, 44 g carbohydrate, 3 g fat (1 g saturated), 2 mg cholesterol, 1,315 mg sodium.

TOMATO TACTICS

To quickly cut up canned tomatoes, leave them in the can and use kitchen shears or scissors to snip them into small pieces. When a recipe calls for using both the cut-up tomatoes and their juice, there's no need to drain the tomatoes.

ARLIC-SAGE-MARINATED BEEF
POT ROAST (recipe, page 55)

Beef & PORK

Contents

Garlic Steaks with Nectarine-Onion Relish

What's better than the smell of steak on the grill in the summertime? The aroma of garlic-studded beef on the grill. Serve this steak with some crusty bread to soak up the delicious juices.

4 boneless beef top loin steaks, cut
    1 inch thick
6 cloves garlic, thinly sliced
2 medium onions, coarsely chopped
1 teaspoon olive oil
2 tablespoons cider vinegar
1 tablespoon honey
1 medium nectarine, chopped
2 teaspoons snipped fresh applemint,
    pineapplemint, or spearmint
    Fresh applemint, pineapplemint,
    or spearmint sprigs (optional)

Trim fat from steaks. With the point of a paring knife, make small slits in steaks. Insert half of the garlic slices into slits.

Wrap the steaks in plastic wrap; let stand at room temperature up to 20 minutes. (For more intense flavor, chill steaks up to 8 hours.) Sprinkle the steaks with salt and pepper.

Meanwhile, for relish, in a large nonstick skillet cook onions and remaining garlic in hot oil over medium heat about 10 minutes or until onions are a deep golden color (but not brown), stirring occasionally. Stir in vinegar and honey. Stir in nectarine and the snipped mint. Heat through.

Grill steaks on an uncovered grill directly over medium coals to desired doneness, turning once. (Allow 8 to 12 minutes for medium rare or 12 to 15 minutes for medium.) Serve the relish with steaks. If desired, garnish with mint sprigs. Makes 4 servings.

Nutrition information per serving: 272 calories, 34 g protein, 13 g carbohydrate, 9 g fat (3 g saturated), 97 mg cholesterol, 108 mg sodium.

OLIVE OIL OPTIONS

All olive oils are not the same. This versatile oil, made from pressed olives, is sold by grade from "pure" (a blend of lower- and higher-quality oils) to "extra virgin" (the richest in aroma and flavor). Color also indicates a flavor difference. Green to greenish gold olive oil tastes slightly sharp. Golden olive oil has a more delicate flavor.

Oriental Family Steak

Oriental Family Steak

To ensure a tender steak, marinate the meat at least 8 hours, and slice it as thin as you can.

1	1½- to 2-pound beef top round steak, cut 1 inch thick
⅓	cup soy sauce
⅓	cup dry sherry
2	green onions, thinly sliced
1	tablespoon brown sugar
1	clove garlic, minced
½	teaspoon dry mustard
⅛	teaspoon ground ginger
	Soy sauce (optional)

Trim fat from meat. Place meat in a plastic bag and set the bag into a shallow dish. For marinade, combine ⅓ cup soy sauce, sherry, green onions, brown sugar, garlic, mustard, and ginger. Pour over meat; seal bag. Marinate in the refrigerator for 8 to 24 hours, turning bag occasionally. Drain meat, reserving marinade.

In a covered grill arrange medium-hot coals around a drip pan. Test for medium heat above pan. Place meat on grill rack over drip pan. Cover and grill to desired doneness. (Allow 24 to 26 minutes for medium rare or 28 to 30 minutes for medium.) Brush occasionally with marinade up to the last 5 minutes of grilling.

Cut the meat into thin slices. If desired, serve with additional soy sauce. Makes 6 to 8 servings.

Nutrition information per serving: 185 calories, 28 g protein, 3 g carbohydrate, 5 g fat (2 g saturated), 72 mg cholesterol, 512 mg sodium.

Herb-Pepper Sirloin Steak

A mixture of catsup, herbs, and pepper coats both sides of this steak, complementing the hearty beef flavor.

1	1½-pound boneless beef sirloin steak, cut 1 inch thick
2	tablespoons catsup
1½	teaspoons snipped fresh rosemary or ½ teaspoon dried rosemary, crushed
1½	teaspoons snipped fresh basil or ½ teaspoon dried basil, crushed
½	teaspoon coarsely ground pepper
⅛	teaspoon garlic powder
⅛	teaspoon ground cardamom (optional)

Trim fat from steak. Combine catsup, rosemary, basil, pepper, garlic powder, and, if desired, cardamom. Coat both sides of steak with catsup mixture.

Grill steak on an uncovered grill directly over medium coals to desired doneness, turning once. (Allow 14 to 18 minutes for medium rare or 18 to 22 minutes for medium.) Cut steak into serving-size pieces. Makes 6 servings.

Nutrition information per serving: 208 calories, 26 g protein, 2 g carbohydrate, 10 g fat (4 g saturated), 76 mg cholesterol, 124 mg sodium.

Midwest Swiss Steak with Tomato Gravy

Serve this satisfying entrée with a tossed green salad and crusty sourdough rolls.

1½ pounds boneless beef round steak
2 tablespoons all-purpose flour
 Nonstick spray coating
2 large onions, sliced
2 cups chopped peeled parsnips
1 14½-ounce can low-sodium
  tomatoes, cut up
1 large red sweet pepper, chopped
1 cup beef broth
1 teaspoon salt-free seasoning blend
1 teaspoon dried basil, crushed
1 clove garlic, minced
¼ teaspoon black pepper
1 tablespoon cold water
1 teaspoon cornstarch
2 tablespoons snipped parsley

Trim fat from meat. Cut the meat into 6 serving-size pieces. Sprinkle both sides of the meat with flour. With a meat mallet, pound the flour into the meat.

Spray an unheated 12-inch skillet with nonstick coating. Preheat over medium heat. Add meat and cook until brown on both sides. Add the onions, parsnips, undrained tomatoes, sweet pepper, beef broth, seasoning blend, basil, garlic, and black pepper.

Bring to boiling; reduce heat. Cover and simmer about 1¼ hours or until meat and vegetables are tender. Transfer meat and vegetables to a platter. Cover and keep warm while preparing sauce.

For sauce, skim fat from pan drippings. Stir together water and cornstarch. Stir into pan drippings. Cook and stir until thickened and bubbly. Cook and stir for 2 minutes more. Stir in parsley. Serve sauce over meat and vegetables. Makes 6 servings.

Nutrition information per serving: 211 calories, 25 g protein, 16 g carbohydrate, 5 g fat (2 g saturated), 60 mg cholesterol, 321 mg sodium.

Snipping savvy

Snipping parsley and other fresh herbs takes only a few moments. Loosely pack the cleaned and dried leaves in a glass measuring cup. Use kitchen shears to cut them into small uniform pieces. This method eliminates the work of washing a cutting board.

Garlic-Sage-Marinated Beef Pot Roast

Red wine, tomato paste, and garlic give this fork-tender roast a robust, well-rounded flavor.

1	2- to 2½-pound boneless beef chuck pot roast
¾	cup dry red wine or tomato juice
2	tablespoons tomato paste
1	tablespoon snipped fresh sage or ½ teaspoon ground sage
10	cloves garlic, halved
2	teaspoons instant beef bouillon granules
¼	teaspoon pepper
1	tablespoon cooking oil
1¼	pounds tiny new potatoes or 4 medium potatoes
4	medium carrots, cut into 2-inch pieces
2	small onions, cut into wedges
2	stalks celery, bias-sliced into 1-inch pieces
½	cup cold water
¼	cup all-purpose flour

Trim fat from meat. Place meat in a plastic bag and set the bag into a shallow dish. For marinade, in a small bowl combine the red wine or tomato juice, tomato paste, sage, garlic, beef bouillon granules, and pepper. Pour over meat; seal bag. Marinate in the refrigerator for 6 to 24 hours, turning bag occasionally. Drain meat, reserving the marinade.

In a Dutch oven brown the meat on both sides in hot oil. Drain fat. Pour the marinade over meat. Bring to boiling; reduce heat. Cover and simmer for 1 hour.

Remove a narrow strip of peel from around the center of each new potato. (Or, peel and quarter each medium potato.) Add potatoes, carrots, onions, and celery to meat. Cover and simmer for 45 to 60 minutes or until meat and vegetables are tender, adding some water if necessary. Transfer meat and vegetables to a platter. Cover and keep warm while preparing gravy.

For gravy, measure pan juices; skim fat. If necessary, add water to equal 1¾ cups liquid; return to Dutch oven. Combine the ½ cup water and flour; stir into juices. Cook and stir until thickened and bubbly. Cook and stir for 1 minute more. Season to taste with salt and pepper. Serve gravy with meat and vegetables. Makes 8 servings.

Nutrition information per serving: 321 calories, 29 g protein, 28 g carbohydrate, 8 g fat (3 g saturated), 78 mg cholesterol, 345 mg sodium.

Beef Fajitas

For chicken fajitas, substitute skinless, boneless chicken breast halves for the flank steak.

1 1½-pound beef flank steak
¼ cup lime juice
2 tablespoons soy sauce
1 tablespoon cooking oil
1 clove garlic, minced
1 avocado, seeded, peeled, and
   coarsely chopped
¼ cup salsa
1 tablespoon snipped cilantro
1 tablespoon lime juice
¼ teaspoon bottled hot pepper sauce
12 8-inch flour tortillas
2 medium onions, sliced
2 medium green sweet peppers,
   cut into strips
1 tablespoon cooking oil
½ cup dairy sour cream
1 medium tomato, coarsely chopped
   (optional)

Trim fat from meat. Score meat by making shallow diagonal cuts at 1-inch intervals in a diamond pattern. Repeat on other side. Place meat in a plastic bag and set the bag into a shallow dish.

For marinade, in a small bowl combine ¼ cup lime juice, soy sauce, 1 tablespoon oil, and garlic. Pour over meat; seal bag. Marinate in the refrigerator for 6 to 12 hours, turning bag occasionally. Toss together the avocado, salsa, cilantro, 1 tablespoon lime juice, and pepper sauce. Cover and chill. Wrap tortillas in foil.

Fold a 36x18-inch piece of heavy foil in half to make an 18-inch square. Place onions and green peppers in center of foil. Drizzle with 1 tablespoon oil. Bring up two opposite edges of foil and seal with a double fold. Then fold remaining ends to completely enclose the vegetables, leaving space for steam to build.

Grill vegetable packet on an uncovered grill directly over medium coals for 10 minutes. Drain the meat, reserving marinade. Add the meat to grill.

Grill meat and vegetable packet for 6 minutes. Brush the meat with marinade; turn meat. Add the wrapped tortillas to grill. Grill for 6 to 8 minutes more or until meat is slightly pink in center and vegetables are crisp-tender.

To serve, thinly slice meat across the grain. Arrange meat, onions, and peppers on tortillas. Top with the avocado mixture, sour cream, and, if desired, tomato. Roll up tortillas around filling. Makes 6 servings.

Nutrition information per serving: 539 calories, 30 g protein, 49 g carbohydrate, 25 g fat (6 g saturated), 61 mg cholesterol, 604 mg sodium.

Sweet-and-Sour Steak

The sweet-and-sour dishes of Canton are among the most familiar types of Chinese food. They are said to have evolved in response to the demanding tastes of the foreigners in this large port city.

8 ounces beef top round steak
1 small orange
1 15¼-ounce can pineapple chunks (juice pack)
2 tablespoons vinegar
2 tablespoons soy sauce
1 tablespoon cornstarch
1 tablespoon brown sugar
⅛ teaspoon ground red pepper
1 tablespoon cooking oil
1 medium green sweet pepper, cut into 1-inch pieces
1 small onion, cut into thin wedges
2 cups hot cooked rice
Orange slices (optional)

Trim fat from meat. Partially freeze meat. Thinly slice across the grain into bite-size strips. Set aside. Peel and section orange. Set aside.

For sauce, drain pineapple, reserving juice. Pour ½ cup of the reserved juice into a small bowl. (Reserve remaining juice for another use.) Stir in the vinegar, soy sauce, cornstarch, brown sugar, and ground red pepper. Set aside.

Add cooking oil to a wok or large skillet. Preheat over medium-high heat (add more oil if necessary during cooking). Stir-fry green pepper and onion in hot oil for 3 to 4 minutes or until crisp-tender. Remove the vegetables from wok.

Add meat to wok. Stir-fry for 2 to 3 minutes or until meat is slightly pink in center. Push meat from center of wok. Stir sauce; add to center of wok. Cook and stir until thickened and bubbly.

Return cooked vegetables to wok. Add pineapple chunks. Stir all ingredients together to coat. Cook and stir about 2 minutes more or until heated through. Stir in orange sections. Serve immediately over hot rice. If desired, garnish with orange slices. Makes 4 servings.

Nutrition information per serving: 326 calories, 17 g protein, 51 g carbohydrate, 7 g fat (2 g saturated fat), 36 mg cholesterol, 545 mg sodium.

Southwest Beef-Linguine Toss

A jar of picante sauce makes an easy, yet flavor-packed sauce in this one-dish meal.

4	ounces packaged dried linguine
12	ounces beef top round steak
1	tablespoon cooking oil
2	teaspoons chili powder
1	clove garlic, minced
1	small onion, sliced and separated into rings
1	red or green sweet pepper, cut into strips
1	10-ounce package frozen whole kernel corn
¼	cup picante sauce
	Cilantro sprigs (optional)

Cook pasta according to package directions. Drain pasta; rinse with warm water. Drain again. Meanwhile, trim fat from meat. Cut meat into thin, bite-size strips.

Add cooking oil to a wok or large skillet. Preheat over medium-high heat (add more oil if necessary during cooking). Stir-fry chili powder and garlic in hot oil for 15 seconds. Add onion; stir-fry for 1 minute. Add sweet pepper; stir-fry for 1 to 2 minutes more or until vegetables are crisp-tender. Remove from wok.

Add meat to wok. Stir-fry for 2 to 3 minutes or until meat is slightly pink in center. Return vegetables to wok. Stir in corn and picante sauce. Add the cooked pasta. Toss all ingredients together to coat. Cook and stir until heated through. Serve immediately. If desired, garnish with cilantro. Makes 4 servings.

Nutrition information per serving: 351 calories, 27 g protein, 43 g carbohydrate, 9 g fat (2 g saturated fat), 54 mg cholesterol, 166 mg sodium.

STIR-FRYING GARLIC

To evenly distribute garlic flavor to stir-fry ingredients, season the oil by cooking the garlic first. Cook the garlic in the hot oil, keeping it moving constantly so it doesn't burn. After about 15 seconds, begin adding the other stir-fry ingredients to the oil.

Fusilli with Creamy Tomato and Meat Sauce

Whipping cream enriches this herbed tomato and meat sauce. Serve it over your favorite pasta strands.

12 ounces lean ground beef or ground
    raw turkey
1 large onion, chopped (1 cup)
2 cloves garlic, minced
2 14½-ounce cans peeled Italian-style
    tomatoes, cut up
1 teaspoon dried Italian seasoning,
    crushed
½ teaspoon sugar
¼ teaspoon salt
⅛ teaspoon pepper
8 ounces packaged dried fusilli,
    vermicelli, or spaghetti
½ cup whipping cream
2 tablespoons snipped parsley
    Fresh rosemary sprigs (optional)

For sauce, in a large saucepan cook beef or turkey, onion, and garlic until meat is brown. Drain fat. Stir in the undrained tomatoes, Italian seasoning, sugar, salt, and pepper. Bring to boiling; reduce heat. Simmer, uncovered, about 40 minutes or until most of the liquid has evaporated, stirring occasionally.

Meanwhile, cook the pasta according to package directions. Drain; keep warm.

Gradually stir the whipping cream into the sauce. Heat through, stirring constantly. Remove from heat. Stir in parsley.

Arrange the pasta on dinner plates or a large platter. Spoon the sauce over the pasta. If desired, garnish with fresh rosemary sprigs. Makes 4 servings.

Nutrition information per serving: 523 calories, 26 g protein, 59 g carbohydrate, 21 g fat (10 g saturated), 94 mg cholesterol, 534 mg sodium.

*P*IPING HOT PASTA

To keep pasta warm, return the hot drained pasta to the hot cooking pan and cover it. To avoid overcooking the pasta and to prevent sticking, hold the hot pasta no longer than 10 minutes and stir it once or twice.

Easy Taco Pizza

This hearty south-of-the border pizza is popular with both kids and adults alike.

Cornmeal Pizza Dough
12 ounces lean ground beef
1 cup chopped onion
1 8-ounce can tomato sauce
1 2¼-ounce can sliced pitted ripe olives, drained
1 1¼-ounce envelope taco seasoning mix
2 cups shredded cheddar cheese (8 ounces)
2 cups shredded lettuce
2 cups chopped tomatoes
2 medium avocados, seeded, peeled, and chopped
1 8-ounce carton dairy sour cream
Chili powder (optional)

Prepare Cornmeal Pizza Dough. Grease two 11- to 13-inch pizza pans or baking sheets. On a lightly floured surface, roll each half of dough into a circle 1 inch larger than pizza pan. Transfer dough to pans. Build up edges slightly. If desired, flute edges. Prick crusts well with a fork. Do not let rise. Bake in a 425° oven for 10 to 12 minutes or until crusts are lightly browned.

Meanwhile, in a large skillet cook ground beef and onion until meat is brown and onion is tender. Drain fat. Stir in tomato sauce, olives, and taco seasoning mix. Heat through.

Spread meat mixture over hot crusts. Sprinkle with cheese. Bake about 12 minutes more or until cheese is melted. Top with lettuce, tomatoes, avocados, and sour cream. If desired, sprinkle sour cream with chili powder. Makes 6 servings.

Cornmeal Pizza Dough: In a large bowl combine 1¼ cups *all-purpose flour,* 1 package *active dry yeast,* and ¼ teaspoon *salt.* Add 1 cup *warm water* (120° to 130°) and 2 tablespoons *cooking oil.* Beat with an electric mixer on low speed for 30 seconds. Beat on high speed for 3 minutes. Using a spoon, stir in ¾ cup *yellow cornmeal* and as much of ¾ to 1¼ cups additional *all-purpose flour* as you can. On a lightly floured surface, knead in enough of the remaining flour to make a moderately stiff dough that is smooth and elastic (6 to 8 minutes total). Divide in half. Cover and let rest for 10 minutes.

Nutrition information per serving: 726 calories, 32 g protein, 56 g carbohydrate, 45 g fat (15 g saturated), 90 mg cholesterol, 1,274 mg sodium.

Chili Macaroni

Wagon wheel macaroni and green beans replace the kidney beans in this chili-style dish.

12	ounces lean ground beef or ground raw turkey
1	medium onion, chopped (½ cup)
1	14½-ounce can Mexican-style stewed tomatoes
1¼	cups tomato juice
2	tablespoons canned diced green chile peppers, drained
2	teaspoons chili powder
½	teaspoon garlic salt
1	cup packaged dried wagon wheel macaroni or elbow macaroni
1	cup loose-pack frozen cut green beans
1	cup shredded cheddar cheese (4 ounces)

In a large skillet cook the ground beef or turkey and onion until meat is brown. Drain fat.

Stir stewed tomatoes, tomato juice, chile peppers, chili powder, and garlic salt into the meat mixture. Bring to boiling. Stir in pasta and green beans. Return to boiling; reduce heat. Cover and simmer about 15 minutes or until pasta and beans are tender.

To serve, spoon into bowls. Sprinkle each serving with shredded cheddar cheese. Makes 4 servings.

Nutrition information per serving: 427 calories, 29 g protein, 32 g carbohydrate, 21 g fat (10 g saturated), 83 mg cholesterol, 1,118 mg sodium.

SELECTING GROUND BEEF

For lower-fat cooking, choose the leanest ground beef possible. Ground beef can range in fat from 75 percent lean (25 percent fat) to 97 percent lean (3 percent fat). For soups, stews, tacos, or casseroles, use 95 to 97 percent lean ground beef. Because very lean ground beef tends to crumble and be less juicy, you may want to use ground beef with slightly more fat for meat loaves, burgers, and meatballs.

Mustard-Orange Pork Tenderloin

A mixture of vegetables, such as cut-up red onions, baby carrots, and chunks of zucchini, can be roasted alongside the meat. Just spray the vegetables with olive oil-flavored nonstick spray coating before placing them in the pan around the meat.

12 ounces pork tenderloin
½ cup apricot preserves or orange marmalade
3 tablespoons Dijon-style mustard
Nonstick spray coating
2 cups sliced fresh mushrooms
½ cup sliced green onions
2 tablespoons orange juice

Trim fat from meat. Place meat on a rack in a shallow roasting pan. Insert a meat thermometer into the center of meat. Roast, uncovered, in a 425° oven for 10 minutes.

Meanwhile, in a small bowl stir together preserves or marmalade and mustard. Spoon half of the mustard mixture over the meat. Set the remaining mustard mixture aside.

Roast for 15 to 25 minutes more or until the meat thermometer registers 155°. Transfer the meat to a warm platter and cover with foil. Let stand for 10 minutes before slicing. (The meat's temperature will rise 5° during standing.)

Meanwhile, spray a medium saucepan with nonstick coating. Add mushrooms and green onions. Cook and stir for 2 to 3 minutes or until mushrooms are tender. Stir in the remaining mustard mixture and orange juice. Cook and stir until heated through.

To serve, thinly slice the meat. Spoon the mushroom mixture over meat. Makes 4 servings.

Nutrition information per serving: 240 calories, 21 g protein, 32 g carbohydrate, 4 g fat (1 g saturated), 60 mg cholesterol, 334 mg sodium.

Cashew Pork and Broccoli

The Portuguese brought the cashew from the New World to India and East Africa in the fifteenth century. From there it traveled to China and worked its way into Chinese cuisine.

12 ounces lean boneless pork
 2 tablespoons soy sauce
 2 teaspoons toasted sesame oil
 2 teaspoons grated gingerroot
 2 cloves garlic, minced
 ½ cup hoisin sauce
 ½ cup water
 2 tablespoons soy sauce
 1 tablespoon cornstarch
 1 teaspoon sugar
 ⅛ teaspoon crushed red pepper
 1 tablespoon cooking oil
 2 medium onions, cut into thin
     wedges
 2 stalks celery, thinly bias-sliced
 3 cups broccoli flowerets
 2 cups hot cooked rice
 ½ cup dry roasted cashews

Trim fat from meat. Partially freeze the meat. Thinly slice across the grain into bite-size strips. In a medium bowl combine the meat strips, 2 tablespoons soy sauce, sesame oil, gingerroot, and garlic. Cover and chill for 1 to 2 hours.

For sauce, in a small mixing bowl stir together the hoisin sauce, water, 2 tablespoons soy sauce, cornstarch, sugar, and crushed red pepper. Set aside.

Add cooking oil to a wok or large skillet. Preheat over medium-high heat (add more oil if necessary during cooking.) Stir-fry onions and celery in hot oil for 1 minute. Add broccoli; stir-fry for 3 to 4 minutes or until crisp-tender. Remove vegetables from wok.

Add meat mixture to wok. Stir-fry for 2 to 3 minutes or until meat is slightly pink in center. Push meat from center of wok.

Stir sauce; add to center of wok. Cook and stir until thickened and bubbly. Return cooked vegetables to wok. Stir all ingredients together to coat. Cover and cook about 1 minute more or until heated through. Serve immediately with hot cooked rice. Sprinkle with cashews. Makes 4 servings.

Nutrition information per serving: 480 calories, 21 g protein, 42 g carbohydrate, 26 g fat (5 g saturated fat), 38 mg cholesterol, 1,554 mg sodium.

Down-Home Ribs

Down-Home Ribs

Fresh gingerroot adds an enticing bite to the sauce. Store extra gingerroot in an air-tight container in your freezer and then just grate as needed.

1	medium onion, chopped
1	tablespoon cooking oil
⅓	cup catsup
2	tablespoons orange juice
1	tablespoon brown sugar
1	teaspoon chili powder
½	teaspoon grated gingerroot
4	pounds pork loin back ribs or meaty spareribs

For sauce, in a medium skillet cook onion in hot oil over medium heat about 4 minutes or until onion is tender. Stir in catsup, orange juice, brown sugar, chili powder, and gingerroot. Cook about 5 minutes more or until sauce is slightly thickened. Remove from heat. Trim fat from ribs. Cut ribs into serving-size pieces.

In a covered grill arrange medium-hot coals around a drip pan. Test for medium heat above the pan. Place the ribs on grill rack over drip pan. Cover and grill for 1¼ to 1½ hours or until ribs are tender. Brush occasionally with sauce during the last 10 minutes of grilling. Makes 6 servings.

Nutrition information per serving: 313 calories, 19 g protein, 8 g carbohydrate, 22 g fat (8 g saturated), 79 mg cholesterol, 245 mg sodium.

Sweet and Tangy Country-Style Ribs

Serve this summertime classic with other picnic favorites, such as corn on the cob and coleslaw.

½	cup chili sauce
2	tablespoons apple jelly
1	tablespoon vinegar
1	teaspoon prepared mustard
1	teaspoon Worcestershire sauce
¼	teaspoon chili powder
2	to 2½ pounds pork country-style ribs

For sauce, in a small saucepan cook and stir chili sauce and jelly until jelly is melted. Stir in vinegar, mustard, Worcestershire sauce, and chili powder. Remove from heat. Trim fat from ribs.

In a covered grill arrange medium-hot coals around a drip pan. Test for medium heat above the pan. Place ribs on grill rack over drip pan. Cover and grill for 1½ to 2 hours or until ribs are tender. Brush occasionally with sauce during the last 15 minutes of grilling. Serve with any remaining sauce. Makes 4 servings.

Nutrition information per serving: 449 calories, 33 g protein, 15 g carbohydrate, 28 g fat (10 g saturated), 129 mg cholesterol, 533 mg sodium.

Ham, Spinach, and Mostaccioli Casserole

Just before serving, be sure to give the casserole a good stir to distribute the rich and creamy sauce.

8 ounces packaged dried mostaccioli, cut ziti, or elbow macaroni
3 tablespoons margarine or butter
3 medium onions, cut into thin wedges, or 5 medium leeks, sliced
2 cloves garlic, minced
¼ cup all-purpose flour
½ teaspoon dried thyme, crushed
⅛ teaspoon pepper
1½ cups half-and-half, light cream, or milk
1½ cups chicken broth
1½ cups cubed fully cooked ham
1 10-ounce package frozen chopped spinach, thawed and drained

Cook pasta according to package directions. Drain pasta; rinse with cold water. Drain again.

In a large saucepan melt margarine or butter. Add onions or leeks and garlic. Cover and cook about 5 minutes or until onions are tender, stirring occasionally. Stir in flour, thyme, and pepper. Add half-and-half, light cream, or milk and the chicken broth all at once. Cook and stir until thickened and bubbly. Cook and stir for 1 minute more. Stir in pasta, ham, and spinach. Spoon mixture into a 3-quart casserole.

Cover and bake in a 350° oven for 30 to 35 minutes or until heated through. Let stand for 5 minutes. Stir gently before serving. Makes 6 servings.

Nutrition information per serving: 388 calories, 18 g protein, 44 g carbohydrate, 16 g fat (6 g saturated), 42 mg cholesterol, 719 mg sodium.

⊺HAWING SPINACH

When you forget to thaw frozen spinach ahead of time, place the unwrapped frozen block of spinach in a colander and run hot water over it, breaking up the block with a fork. If you prefer, you can micro-thaw spinach by placing the unwrapped block in a bowl and micro-cooking it on 30% power (medium-low) for 2 to 4 minutes or until soft enough to break into chunks. Continue to cook the spinach on 30% power for 3 to 5 minutes or until thawed.

Italian Pizza Sandwiches

Some like it hot! If you do, choose the hot sausage. For those with less adventurous palates, choose the mild or sweet sausage. You may want to grill some of each.

1 medium green sweet pepper, cut into thin strips
1 medium onion, thinly sliced
1 tablespoon margarine or butter
4 uncooked mild or hot Italian sausage links (12 to 16 ounces total)
½ cup pizza sauce
4 individual French-style rolls, split
2 tablespoons grated Parmesan cheese

Fold a 36x18-inch piece of heavy foil in half to make an 18-inch square. Place green pepper and onion in the center of the foil. Dot with margarine or butter.

Bring up two opposite edges of foil and seal with a double fold. Then fold remaining ends to completely enclose vegetables, leaving space for steam to build. Prick the sausage links in several places with a fork or the tip of a sharp knife.

In a covered grill arrange medium-hot coals around a drip pan. Test for medium heat above the pan. Place sausage links and vegetable packet on grill rack over drip pan. Cover and grill for 20 to 25 minutes or until sausage juices run clear and vegetables are tender.

Meanwhile, in a small saucepan heat pizza sauce. Toast cut sides of French rolls on grill.

To serve, halve the sausage links lengthwise, cutting to, but not through, the other side. Place sausage links in the toasted rolls. Top with the grilled vegetables and warm pizza sauce. Sprinkle with Parmesan cheese. Makes 4 servings.

Nutrition information per serving: 376 calories, 18 g protein, 26 g carbohydrate, 22 g fat (7 g saturated), 51 mg cholesterol, 1,067 mg sodium.

Bow Ties with Sausage & Peppers

You will be amazed that so few ingredients generate so much flavor. To reduce the fat, use Italian-style ground turkey sausage.

8	ounces packaged dried large bow-tie pasta
12	ounces spicy Italian sausage links
2	medium red sweet peppers, cut into ¾-inch pieces
½	cup vegetable broth or beef broth
¼	teaspoon coarsely ground black pepper
¼	cup snipped Italian flat-leaf parsley

Cook pasta according to package directions. Drain; keep warm. Meanwhile, cut the sausage into 1-inch pieces. In a large skillet cook sausage and sweet peppers over medium-high heat until sausage is brown. Drain fat.

Stir the vegetable or beef broth and black pepper into sausage mixture. Bring to boiling; reduce heat. Simmer, uncovered, for 5 minutes. Remove from heat. Pour the sausage mixture over pasta; add parsley. Toss gently to coat. Makes 4 servings.

Nutrition information per serving: 397 calories, 24 g protein, 38 g carbohydrate, 18 g fat (6 g saturated), 94 mg cholesterol, 713 mg sodium.

Greek-Style Pasta Skillet

Lamb, cinnamon, and feta cheese add a Greek twist to this macaroni casserole.

12	ounces ground lamb or lean ground beef
1	medium onion, chopped (½ cup)
1	14½-ounce can diced tomatoes
1	5½-ounce can tomato juice
½	cup water
½	teaspoon instant beef bouillon granules
½	teaspoon ground cinnamon
⅛	teaspoon garlic powder
1	cup packaged dried medium shell macaroni or elbow macaroni
1	cup loose-pack frozen cut green beans
½	cup crumbled feta cheese

In a large skillet cook ground meat and onion until meat is brown. Drain fat. Stir in the undrained tomatoes, tomato juice, water, bouillon granules, cinnamon, and garlic powder.

Bring to boiling. Stir the uncooked pasta and green beans into meat mixture. Return to boiling; reduce heat. Cover and simmer about 15 minutes or until pasta and green beans are tender. Sprinkle with feta cheese. Makes 4 servings.

Nutrition information per serving: 362 calories, 22 g protein, 33 g carbohydrate, 16 g fat (7 g saturated fat), 70 mg cholesterol, 647 mg sodium.

Greek-Style Pasta Skillet

Poultry

Contents

MINNESOTA APPLE- AND WILD
RICE STUFFED CHICKEN
(recipe, page 93)

Ruby-Glazed Chicken Breasts

These chicken breasts have such a rich flavor from the currant and apple glaze that you would never guess they are low in fat—only 3 grams per serving.

⅓ cup apple juice
3 tablespoons currant jelly
1 teaspoon cornstarch
¼ teaspoon salt
⅛ teaspoon dried marjoram, crushed
3 whole small chicken breasts
    (about 2¼ pounds total),
    halved lengthwise

For sauce, in a small saucepan combine apple juice, currant jelly, cornstarch, and salt. Cook and stir over medium heat until thickened and bubbly. Cook and stir for 2 minutes more. Remove from heat. Stir in the marjoram. Set aside.

If desired, skin chicken. Rinse chicken; pat dry with paper towels.

Grill chicken, bone side up, on an uncovered grill directly over medium coals for 35 to 45 minutes or until chicken is tender and no longer pink, turning and brushing once with sauce.

(Or, in a covered grill arrange medium-hot coals around a drip pan. Test for medium heat above the pan. Place chicken, bone side down, on grill rack over drip pan. Cover and grill for 50 to 60 minutes. Brush occasionally with sauce during the last 20 minutes of grilling.)

Brush the grilled chicken with any remaining sauce before serving. Makes 6 servings.

Nutrition information per serving: 167 calories, 25 g protein, 9 g carbohydrate, 3 g fat (1 g saturated), 69 mg cholesterol, 150 mg sodium.

Southwest Chicken Breasts

To transform this dish into a salad, slice the chicken breasts and arrange them on plates lined with shredded lettuce.
Top with the avocado mixture for a chunky dressing and add some shredded Monterey Jack cheese.

6 medium skinless, boneless chicken breast halves (about 1½ pounds total)
¼ cup dry white wine
2 tablespoons olive oil or cooking oil
2 teaspoons snipped fresh tarragon or ¼ teaspoon dried tarragon, crushed
¼ teaspoon salt
2 avocados, seeded, peeled, and chopped
1 tomato, chopped
2 green onions, finely chopped
2 tablespoons finely chopped, seeded green chile peppers (such as jalapeño, serrano, or Anaheim)
1 tablespoon snipped cilantro
1 tablespoon honey
1 tablespoon lemon juice
1 clove garlic, minced
Lettuce leaves (optional)

Rinse chicken; pat dry with paper towels. Place chicken in a plastic bag and set the bag into a shallow dish. For marinade, in a small bowl combine the white wine, oil, tarragon, and salt. Pour over chicken; seal bag. Marinate in the refrigerator for 2 to 24 hours, turning bag occasionally.

Meanwhile, combine avocados, tomato, green onions, chile peppers, cilantro, honey, lemon juice, and garlic. Toss gently to mix. Cover and chill up to 2 hours.

Drain chicken, reserving marinade. Grill chicken on an uncovered grill directly over medium coals for 12 to 15 minutes or until tender and no longer pink, turning and brushing once with marinade halfway through grilling.

(Or, in a covered grill arrange medium-hot coals around a drip pan. Test for medium heat above the pan. Place chicken on grill rack over drip pan. Cover and grill for 15 to 18 minutes. Brush occasionally with marinade up to the last 5 minutes of grilling.)

Serve the grilled chicken with avocado mixture and, if desired, lettuce leaves. Makes 6 servings.

Nutrition information per serving: 239 calories, 20 g protein, 5 g carbohydrate, 16 g fat (1 g saturated), 50 mg cholesterol, 130 mg sodium.

Chicken with Apricots and Prunes

Boost the flavor in the rice accompaniment with toasted slivered almonds and snipped parsley.

2 to 2½ pounds meaty chicken pieces (breasts, thighs, and drumsticks)
½ teaspoon salt
½ teaspoon garlic powder
¼ teaspoon pepper
2 tablespoons cooking oil
1 6-ounce package dried apricots
1 cup pitted prunes, cut into halves
1 cup chicken broth
¾ cup dry white wine
¼ cup white wine vinegar
1 tablespoon brown sugar
3 inches stick cinnamon
4 whole cloves
3 tablespoons Dijon-style mustard
3 tablespoons water
4 teaspoons all-purpose flour
Hot cooked rice
Thinly sliced green onion (optional)

If desired, skin chicken. Rinse chicken; pat dry with paper towels. Sprinkle chicken with salt, garlic powder, and pepper.

In a 4½-quart Dutch oven cook chicken in hot cooking oil over medium heat about 15 minutes or until lightly browned, turning to brown evenly. Drain fat.

Add apricots, prunes, chicken broth, white wine, wine vinegar, brown sugar, cinnamon, and cloves. Bring to boiling; reduce heat. Cover and simmer for 35 to 40 minutes or until chicken is tender and no longer pink.

Using a slotted spoon, transfer the chicken and fruit to a serving platter; keep warm. Discard cinnamon and cloves. For sauce, in a small bowl stir together the Dijon mustard, water, and flour. Stir into the broth mixture. Cook and stir until thickened and bubbly. Cook and stir for 1 minute more.

Serve chicken and fruit over cooked rice. Top with some of the sauce. If desired, garnish with sliced green onion. Pass the remaining sauce. Makes 6 servings.

Nutrition information per serving: 570 calories, 29 g protein, 82 g carbohydrate, 13 g fat (3 g saturated), 69 mg cholesterol, 580 mg sodium.

Texas-Style Barbecued Chicken Legs

Cut lengthwise strips of assorted sweet peppers and grill to perfection alongside the chicken.

1 medium onion, finely chopped (½ cup)
2 cloves garlic, minced
1 teaspoon chili powder
¼ teaspoon ground sage
1 tablespoon margarine or butter
½ cup catsup
2 tablespoons water
2 tablespoons vinegar
1 tablespoon sugar
1 tablespoon lemon juice
1 tablespoon Worcestershire sauce
½ teaspoon salt
½ teaspoon bottled hot pepper sauce
¼ teaspoon cracked black pepper
6 chicken legs (thigh-drumstick pieces) (3 to 3½ pounds total)

For sauce, in a small saucepan cook onion, garlic, chili powder, and sage in margarine or butter until onion is tender. Stir in catsup, water, vinegar, sugar, lemon juice, Worcestershire sauce, salt, hot pepper sauce, and black pepper. Bring to boiling; reduce heat. Simmer, uncovered, for 5 minutes, stirring occasionally.

Meanwhile, rinse chicken; pat dry with paper towels. Grill chicken, skin side down, on an uncovered grill directly over medium coals for 35 to 40 minutes or until chicken is tender and no longer pink, turning once. (Or, place chicken on the unheated rack of a broiler pan. Broil 5 to 6 inches from the heat for 28 to 32 minutes, turning once.) Brush with sauce during the last 10 minutes of grilling or broiling.

Heat the remaining sauce until bubbly. Pass the sauce with chicken. Makes 6 servings.

Nutrition information per serving: 276 calories, 25 g protein, 11 g carbohydrate, 15 g fat (4 g saturated), 86 mg cholesterol, 596 mg sodium.

TEST THE TEMPERATURE

Before you grill, check the temperature of the coals. Hold your hand, palm side down, in the location you plan to place the food. Count "one thousand one, one thousand two," etc., for as long as you can hold your hand there. Two seconds means the coals are hot, three is medium-hot, four is medium, five is medium-slow, and six is slow.

Curried Chicken Thighs

You also can use skinless, boneless chicken thighs in this Indian-style recipe. Just reduce the cooking time to 10 minutes after adding the chicken broth.

8   chicken thighs (about 2½ pounds total)
2   tablespoons cooking oil
1   cup sliced fresh mushrooms
1   medium onion, chopped (½ cup)
1   clove garlic, minced
3   to 4 teaspoons curry powder
¼   teaspoon salt
¼   teaspoon ground cinnamon
¾   cup chicken broth
1   medium apple, cored and chopped
1   cup half-and-half, light cream, or milk
2   tablespoons all-purpose flour
3   cups hot cooked rice
    Assorted condiments: raisins, chopped hard-cooked egg, peanuts, chopped tomato, chopped green sweet pepper, toasted coconut, chutney, cut-up fruits (optional)

Skin chicken. Rinse chicken; pat dry with paper towels. In a 10-inch skillet cook chicken in hot oil over medium heat about 10 minutes or until lightly browned, turning to brown evenly. Remove chicken. If necessary, add 1 tablespoon additional cooking oil to skillet.

Add mushrooms, onion, and garlic to skillet; cook until vegetables are tender. Add curry powder, salt, and cinnamon; cook and stir for 1 minute. Add chicken broth and apple. Return chicken to skillet. Bring to boiling; reduce heat. Cover and simmer about 15 minutes or until chicken is tender and no longer pink.

Transfer chicken to platter; keep warm. Stir the half-and-half, light cream, or milk into the flour. Stir into pan juices. Cook and stir until thickened and bubbly. Cook and stir for 1 minute more. Spoon some sauce over chicken. Pass remaining sauce. Serve with rice and, if desired, pass condiments. Makes 4 servings.

Nutrition information per serving: 695 calories, 54 g protein, 45 g carbohydrate, 32 g fat (10 g saturated), 158 mg cholesterol, 829 mg sodium.

Minnesota Apple- and Wild Rice-Stuffed Chicken

Team up this bird with a chicory and red onion salad dressed with a blue cheese vinaigrette.

1 6-ounce package long grain and
   wild rice mix
8 ounces sliced fresh mushrooms
   (3 cups)
2 medium cooking apples (such as
   Granny Smith or Jonathan),
   cored and chopped
1 cup shredded carrot
½ cup thinly sliced green onions
½ teaspoon pepper
1 5- to 6-pound whole roasting
   chicken
2 to 3 tablespoons apple jelly, melted
   Apple wedges (optional)

For stuffing, cook rice according to package directions, except add mushrooms, apples, shredded carrot, green onions, and pepper to rice before cooking.

Meanwhile, rinse chicken; pat dry with paper towels. Spoon some of the stuffing loosely into the neck cavity. Pull neck skin to back; fasten with a small skewer. Lightly spoon the remaining stuffing into the body cavity. Tuck the drumsticks under the band of skin that crosses the tail. If there is no band, tie the drumsticks to tail. Twist the wing tips under the chicken.

Place stuffed chicken, breast side up, on a rack in a shallow roasting pan. Insert meat thermometer into the center of an inside thigh muscle. The bulb should not touch the bone.

Roast, uncovered, in a 325° oven for 1¾ to 2½ hours or until meat thermometer registers 180°. At this time, chicken is no longer pink and the drumsticks move easily in their sockets. When the bird is two-thirds done, cut the band of skin or string between drumsticks so thighs will cook evenly. Brush chicken with melted jelly once or twice during the last 10 minutes of roasting.

Remove the chicken from oven; cover with foil. Let stand for 10 to 20 minutes before carving. Transfer chicken to a serving platter. Spoon some of the stuffing around the chicken. If desired, garnish with apple wedges. Pass the remaining stuffing. Makes 10 servings.

Nutrition information per serving: 332 calories, 34 g protein, 19 g carbohydrate, 13 g fat (4 g saturated), 93 mg cholesterol, 365 mg sodium.

Pacific Rim Stir-Fry

Adjust the hotness of this stir-fry by reducing or increasing the amount of chile oil used.

3 ounces rice sticks (also called rice noodles) or packaged dried vermicelli, broken

12 ounces skinless, boneless chicken thighs or breast halves

½ cup chicken broth

2 tablespoons snipped fresh basil or 2 teaspoons dried basil, crushed

2 tablespoons soy sauce

2 teaspoons cornstarch

1 teaspoon chile oil or ½ teaspoon crushed red pepper

½ teaspoon ground turmeric

1 tablespoon cooking oil

2 medium carrots, cut into julienne strips

2 cups broccoli flowerets

1 red or green sweet pepper, cut into lengthwise strips

¼ cup cashew halves or peanuts

In a saucepan cook rice sticks in boiling water for 3 minutes. (Or, cook vermicelli according to package directions.) Drain; keep warm.

Meanwhile, rinse chicken; pat dry with paper towels. Cut chicken thighs or breasts into thin, bite-size strips; set aside.

For sauce, in a small bowl combine chicken broth, basil, soy sauce, cornstarch, chile oil or crushed red pepper, and turmeric; set aside.

Add cooking oil to a wok or 12-inch skillet. Preheat over medium-high heat (add more oil if necessary during cooking). Stir-fry carrot strips in hot oil for 1 minute. Add broccoli; stir-fry for 2 minutes. Add sweet pepper strips; stir-fry for 1½ to 3 minutes more or until crisp-tender. Remove from wok. Add the chicken to wok; stir-fry for 2 to 3 minutes or until tender and no longer pink. Push from center of wok.

Stir sauce; add to center of wok. Cook and stir until thickened and bubbly. Return cooked vegetables to wok. Stir all ingredients together to coat. Cook and stir about 2 minutes more or until heated through. Serve immediately over hot rice sticks or vermicelli. Top with cashews or peanuts. Makes 4 servings.

Nutrition information per serving: 309 calories, 17 g protein, 32 g carbohydrate, 13 g fat (3 g saturated), 41 mg cholesterol, 748 mg sodium.

Chicken and Apple Stir-Fry

This sweet-spiced dish includes an array of colorful peppers, plus dried mushrooms, crunchy almonds, and crisp, tart apple slices.

6 dried mushrooms (such as shiitake or wood ear mushrooms)

12 ounces skinless, boneless chicken breast halves or turkey breast tenderloin steaks

¾ cup cold water

3 tablespoons frozen orange, apple, or pineapple juice concentrate, thawed

2 tablespoons soy sauce

2 teaspoons cornstarch

¼ teaspoon ground ginger

¼ teaspoon ground cinnamon

⅛ to ¼ teaspoon ground red pepper

¼ cup sliced or slivered almonds

1 tablespoon cooking oil

2 medium green, red, orange, and/or yellow sweet peppers, cut into thin strips

2 medium apples, thinly sliced

2 cups hot cooked brown rice

In a small bowl cover mushrooms with warm water. Let soak for 30 minutes. Rinse and squeeze the mushrooms to drain thoroughly. Discard stems. Thinly slice mushrooms. Set aside.

Meanwhile, rinse chicken or turkey; pat dry with paper towels. Cut into 1-inch pieces. Set aside.

For sauce, in a small mixing bowl stir together the cold water, juice concentrate, soy sauce, cornstarch, ginger, cinnamon, and ground red pepper. Set aside.

Preheat a wok or large skillet over medium-high heat. Add almonds; stir-fry for 2 to 3 minutes or until golden. Remove almonds from wok. Let wok cool slightly.

Add cooking oil to wok. Preheat over medium-high heat (add more oil if necessary during cooking). Stir-fry mushrooms, sweet peppers, and apples in hot oil for 1 to 2 minutes or until peppers and apples are crisp-tender. Remove apple mixture from wok.

Add chicken to wok. Stir-fry for 3 to 4 minutes or until tender and no longer pink. Push chicken from center of wok. Stir sauce; add to center of wok. Cook and stir until thickened and bubbly. Return apple mixture to wok. Stir all ingredients together to coat. Cook and stir for 1 to 2 minutes more or until heated through.

Stir in toasted almonds. Serve immediately over hot cooked brown rice. Makes 4 servings.

Nutrition information per serving: 370 calories, 22 g protein, 48 g carbohydrate, 11 g fat (2 g saturated fat), 45 mg cholesterol, 563 mg sodium.

Quick Chicken Fajitas

For a delicious one-dish meal, begin with chicken and a few simple ingredients. Round out dinner with scoops of your favorite ice cream or sherbet and raspberries or sliced strawberries.

8　7-inch flour tortillas

12　ounces skinless, boneless chicken breast halves or turkey breast tenderloin steaks

1　tablespoon lime juice or lemon juice

½　teaspoon ground cumin

½　teaspoon ground coriander

¼　teaspoon dried oregano, crushed

¼　cup clear Italian salad dressing (not reduced-fat dressing)

¾　cup red and/or green sweet pepper cut into strips

1　small onion, halved lengthwise and sliced

　　Assorted condiments: salsa, dairy sour cream, guacamole, jalapeño peppers

　　Shredded lettuce (optional)

Wrap tortillas in foil. Heat in a 350° oven for 10 to 15 minutes or until heated through. Or, wrap in paper towels or waxed paper and heat in a microwave oven on 100% power (high) for 15 to 20 seconds.

Meanwhile, rinse chicken or turkey; pat dry with paper towels. Thinly slice chicken or turkey into bite-size strips. In a medium bowl combine lime or lemon juice, cumin, coriander, and oregano. Stir in chicken or turkey; set aside.

In a large skillet heat the salad dressing over medium-high heat. Add chicken mixture. Cook and stir about 2 minutes or until chicken is tender and no longer pink. With a slotted spoon, remove the chicken from skillet.

Add sweet pepper and sliced onion to skillet; cook and stir for 2 to 3 minutes or until vegetables are crisp-tender. Return the chicken to skillet; heat through.

Spoon the chicken mixture onto warm tortillas; roll up. Top with favorite condiments. If desired, serve on a bed of shredded lettuce. Makes 4 servings.

Nutrition information per serving: 425 calories, 23 g protein, 45 g carbohydrate, 17 g fat (4 g saturated fat), 51 mg cholesterol, 600 mg sodium.

Chicken Manicotti with Chive-Cream Sauce

Broccoli and roasted red peppers or pimiento add vivid colors to the tasty chicken filling that spills from these pasta shells.

12 packaged dried manicotti shells
1 8-ounce container soft-style cream cheese with chives and onion
⅔ cup milk
¼ cup grated Romano or Parmesan cheese
2 cups chopped cooked chicken (10 ounces)
1 10-ounce package frozen chopped broccoli, thawed and drained
½ of a 7-ounce jar roasted red sweet peppers, drained and sliced, or one 4-ounce jar diced pimiento, drained
¼ teaspoon black pepper
Paprika

Cook manicotti shells according to package directions. Drain shells; rinse with cold water. Drain again.

Meanwhile, for sauce, in a small heavy saucepan melt cream cheese over medium-low heat, stirring constantly. Slowly add milk, stirring until smooth. Stir in Romano or Parmesan cheese. Remove from heat.

For filling, in a medium mixing bowl stir together ¾ cup of the sauce, chicken, broccoli, roasted red sweet peppers or pimiento, and black pepper. Using a small spoon, carefully fill each manicotti shell with about ⅓ cup of the filling.

Arrange the filled shells in a 3-quart rectangular baking dish. Pour the remaining sauce over the shells. Sprinkle with paprika. Cover with foil. Bake in a 350° oven for 25 to 30 minutes or until heated through. Makes 6 servings.

Nutrition information per serving: 396 calories, 25 g protein, 31 g carbohydrate, 18 g fat (9 g saturated), 92 mg cholesterol, 257 mg sodium.

QUICK-COOKED CHICKEN

If you need cooked chicken for a recipe but don't have any leftovers, one solution is to purchase a deli-roasted chicken. Or, poach chicken breasts. For 2 cups chopped cooked chicken, in a large skillet combine 12 ounces skinless, boneless chicken breast halves and 1½ cups water. Cover and simmer for 12 to 14 minutes or until tender and no longer pink. Drain and cut up chicken.

Deep-Dish Chicken Pie

To save time with the same delicious results, you can easily substitute one folded refrigerated unbaked piecrust for the Pastry for Single-Crust Pie. Just put the chicken mixture in a 2-quart round casserole and top with the piecrust. Flute, brush, and bake as directed in the recipe.

Pastry for Single-Crust Pie
3 medium leeks or 1 large onion, chopped
1 cup sliced fresh mushrooms
¾ cup sliced celery
½ cup chopped red sweet pepper
2 tablespoons margarine or butter
⅓ cup all-purpose flour
1 teaspoon poultry seasoning
¼ teaspoon salt
¼ teaspoon black pepper
1½ cups chicken broth
1 cup half-and-half, light cream, or milk
2½ cups chopped cooked chicken
1 cup frozen peas
1 slightly beaten egg

Prepare Pastry for Single-Crust Pie. On a lightly floured surface, roll pastry into a rectangle ⅛ inch thick. Trim to a rectangle 1 inch larger than a 2-quart rectangular baking dish. Using a sharp knife or small cookie cutter, cut some shapes out of center of pastry.

In a large saucepan cook leeks or onion, mushrooms, celery, and sweet pepper in margarine or butter over medium heat until tender. Stir in the flour, poultry seasoning, salt, and black pepper. Add the broth and half-and-half, light cream, or milk all at once. Cook and stir until thickened and bubbly. Stir in the cooked chicken and peas. Pour into the baking dish.

Place pastry over the hot chicken mixture in dish; turn edges of pastry under and flute to top edges of dish. Brush with the egg. Place reserved pastry shapes on top of pastry. Brush again with egg.

Bake in a 400° oven for 30 to 35 minutes or until the crust is golden brown. Cool about 20 minutes before serving. Makes 6 servings.

Pastry for Single-Crust Pie: In a medium bowl stir together 1¼ cups *all-purpose flour* and ¼ teaspoon *salt*. Using a pastry blender, cut in ⅓ cup *shortening* until pieces are pea-size. Using 4 to 5 tablespoons *cold water*, sprinkle 1 tablespoon water at a time over mixture, gently tossing with a fork until all is moistened. Form dough into a ball.

Nutrition information per serving: 484 calories, 27 g protein, 35 g carbohydrate, 26 g fat (8 g saturated fat), 107 mg cholesterol, 538 mg sodium.

Stuffed Turkey Tenderloins

There's more than one way to stuff a turkey. Fresh spinach and tangy goat cheese make a melt-in-your-mouth filling in these turkey tenderloins. When sliced, the rosy-red, spicy crust on the meat yields to a juicy, tender interior.

2	8-ounce turkey breast tenderloins
2	cups chopped spinach leaves
3	ounces semisoft goat cheese (chèvre) or feta cheese, crumbled (about ¾ cup)
½	teaspoon black pepper
1	tablespoon olive oil
1	teaspoon paprika
½	teaspoon salt
⅛	to ¼ teaspoon ground red pepper

Rinse turkey; pat dry with paper towels. Make a pocket in each tenderloin by cutting lengthwise from one side almost to, but not through, the opposite side. Set aside.

For stuffing, in a medium bowl combine spinach, goat or feta cheese, and black pepper. Spoon stuffing into pockets. Tie 100% cotton string around each tenderloin in 3 or 4 places to hold in stuffing. In a small bowl combine oil, paprika, salt, and ground red pepper. Brush evenly over turkey.

Grill turkey on lightly greased rack of an uncovered grill directly over medium coals for 16 to 20 minutes or until turkey is tender and no longer pink in center of the thickest part, turning once.

Remove and discard the strings. Slice turkey tenderloins crosswise. Makes 4 servings.

Nutrition information per serving: 220 calories, 26 g protein, 1 g carbohydrate, 12 g fat (4 g saturated), 68 mg cholesterol, 458 mg sodium.

*C*LEANING YOUR GRILL

To make the job easier, clean your grill rack right after cooking. Let it cool until easily handled, then soak it in hot sudsy water to loosen cooked-on grime. If the rack is too large for your sink, let it stand about 1 hour wrapped in wet paper towels, then wipe clean. If necessary, use a stiff brush to remove stubborn burned-on food.

Pineapple-Orange Ginger Turkey

This easy-to-fix Polynesian-style dish capitalizes on the tangy-sweet flavors of pineapple and orange juice concentrate plus a generous amount of fresh ginger.

1   pound turkey breast tenderloin
      steaks
2   tablespoons soy sauce
2   tablespoons dry sherry
½   of a 6-ounce can (⅓ cup) frozen
      orange juice concentrate, thawed
2   tablespoons soy sauce
1   tablespoon water
2   teaspoons cornstarch
½   teaspoon sugar
1   tablespoon cooking oil
2   to 3 teaspoons grated gingerroot
1   medium red or green sweet pepper,
      cut into bite-size strips
1   8-ounce can pineapple chunks
      (juice pack), drained
2   cups hot cooked rice
      Orange slices (optional)
      Fresh rosemary sprigs (optional)

Rinse turkey; pat dry with paper towels. Cut into thin bite-size strips. In a medium bowl stir together turkey, 2 tablespoons soy sauce, and sherry. Cover and chill for 30 minutes to 1 hour.

For sauce, in a small bowl stir together the orange juice concentrate, 2 tablespoons soy sauce, water, cornstarch, and sugar. Set aside.

Add cooking oil to a wok or large skillet. Preheat over medium-high heat (add more oil if necessary during cooking). Stir-fry gingerroot in hot oil for 15 seconds. Add pepper strips; stir-fry for 1 to 2 minutes or until crisp-tender. Remove pepper strips from wok.

Add half of the turkey mixture to wok. Stir-fry for 2 to 3 minutes or until turkey is tender and no longer pink. Remove turkey from wok. Repeat with the remaining turkey mixture. Return all of the turkey to wok. Push turkey from center of wok.

Stir sauce; add to center of wok. Cook and stir until thickened and bubbly. Return pepper strips to wok. Add pineapple. Stir all ingredients together to coat. Cook and stir about 1 minute more or until mixture is heated through.

Serve immediately with hot rice. If desired, garnish with orange slices and rosemary. Makes 4 servings.

Nutrition information per serving: 352 calories, 25 g protein, 46 g carbohydrate, 6 g fat (1 g saturated fat), 50 mg cholesterol, 1,077 mg sodium.

Grilled Turkey Burgers

Herbed Turkey and Broccoli

Soft-style cream cheese makes an ultra-rich sauce for this one-pan pasta dish.

8 ounces packaged dried linguine or spaghetti, broken in half
3 cups small broccoli flowerets
1 8-ounce container soft-style cream cheese with garlic and herbs
⅔ cup milk
¼ teaspoon coarsely ground pepper
6 ounces sliced fully cooked smoked turkey breast, cut into bite-size strips

In a 4½-quart Dutch oven cook pasta in boiling water for 6 minutes. Add broccoli. Return to boiling. Cook for 2 to 3 minutes more or until pasta is tender and broccoli is crisp-tender. Drain in a colander.

In the same Dutch oven combine cream cheese, milk, and pepper. Cook and stir over low heat until cream cheese is melted. Add pasta mixture and turkey. Toss to coat. If necessary, stir in additional milk to make desired consistency. Makes 4 servings.

Nutrition information per serving: 516 calories, 25 g protein, 57 g carbohydrate, 21 g fat (11 g saturated), 81 mg cholesterol, 675 mg sodium.

Grilled Turkey Burgers

Who says beef has to make the all-American burger? We gave the classic burger a makeover by using ground turkey, glazing it with orange marmalade, and serving it on rye or wheat buns.

1 beaten egg
⅓ cup fine dry bread crumbs
¼ cup finely chopped green sweet pepper
2 green onions, finely chopped
2 tablespoons milk
½ teaspoon salt
⅛ teaspoon black pepper
1 pound ground raw turkey
2 tablespoons orange marmalade
5 rye or wheat sandwich buns, split
Shredded lettuce (optional)
Tomato slices, halved (optional)
Onion slices (optional)

In a medium mixing bowl combine egg, bread crumbs, green pepper, chopped green onions, milk, salt, and black pepper. Add ground turkey; mix well. Shape mixture into five ¾-inch-thick patties.

Grill patties on an uncovered grill directly over medium coals for 14 to 18 minutes or until done (165°), turning and brushing once with orange marmalade.

(Or, in a covered grill arrange medium-hot coals around a drip pan. Test for medium heat above the pan. Place patties on grill rack over drip pan. Cover and grill for 20 to 24 minutes, turning and brushing once with orange marmalade.)

Toast cut sides of buns on grill. Serve patties in buns and, if desired, with lettuce, tomato, and onion slices. Makes 5 servings.

Nutrition information per serving: 289 calories, 17 g protein, 30 g carbohydrate, 11 g fat (2 g saturated), 77 mg cholesterol, 396 mg sodium.

Spaghetti with Turkey Meatballs

We updated everyone's favorite pasta dish by using ground turkey instead of ground beef.

1 large onion, chopped (1 cup)
1 medium green sweet pepper, coarsely chopped (1 cup)
1 medium carrot, coarsely chopped (½ cup)
1 stalk celery, sliced (½ cup)
1 tablespoon cooking oil
4 large ripe tomatoes, peeled and chopped (4 cups), or two 14½-ounce cans tomatoes, cut up
1 6-ounce can (⅔ cup) tomato paste
2 teaspoons dried Italian seasoning, crushed
½ teaspoon sugar
½ teaspoon salt
½ teaspoon garlic powder
  Turkey Meatballs
12 ounces packaged dried spaghetti or mostaccioli

For sauce, in a Dutch oven cook onion, green pepper, carrot, and celery in hot oil until tender. Stir in fresh or undrained canned tomatoes, tomato paste, Italian seasoning, sugar, salt, and garlic powder. Bring to boiling.

Add the Turkey Meatballs; reduce heat. Cover and simmer for 30 minutes. If necessary, uncover and simmer for 10 to 15 minutes more or until sauce is desired consistency, stirring occasionally.

Meanwhile, cook the pasta according to package directions. Drain.

Arrange pasta on individual plates or a large platter. Spoon the meatballs and sauce over pasta. Makes 6 servings.

Turkey Meatballs: In a medium mixing bowl combine 1 beaten *egg* and 2 tablespoons *milk*. Stir in ¼ cup *fine dry bread crumbs;* ½ teaspoon *salt;* ½ teaspoon *dried Italian seasoning,* crushed; and ½ teaspoon *pepper.* Add 1 pound *ground raw turkey;* mix well. With wet hands, shape mixture into twenty-four 1-inch meatballs. Place the meatballs in a greased 13x9x2-inch baking pan. Bake in a 375° oven about 20 minutes or until turkey is done (165°). Drain fat.

Nutrition information per serving: 442 calories, 22 g protein, 65 g carbohydrate, 11 g fat (2 g saturated), 64 mg cholesterol, 686 mg sodium.

HALIBUT WITH CREAMY DIJON SAUCE
(recipe, page 119)

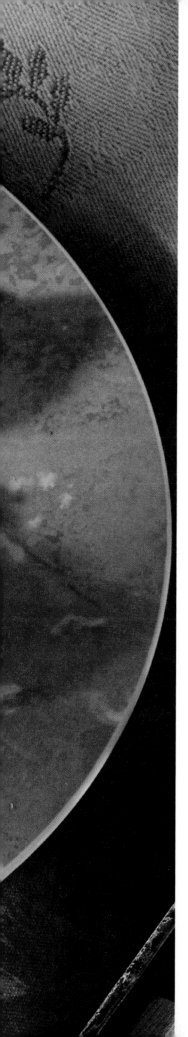

Fish & SEAFOOD

Contents

Poached Orange Roughy with Lemon Sauce

Despite its speed, poaching is an inherently gentle way to cook. It's also one of the lightest and most healthful. Here, poaching in lemon- and pepper-infused broth preserves the delicate flavor and texture of one of the most popular kinds of white fish.

1 pound fresh or frozen orange roughy or red snapper fillets, about ½ inch thick
1 pound asparagus
1 14½-ounce can reduced-sodium chicken broth
2 teaspoons finely shredded lemon peel
⅛ teaspoon black pepper
1 medium yellow sweet pepper, cut into bite-size strips
4 teaspoons cornstarch
2 tablespoons snipped fresh chives
2 cups hot cooked couscous or rice

Thaw fish, if frozen. Rinse fish. Cut the fish into 4 serving-size portions; set aside. Snap off and discard woody bases from asparagus. Cut asparagus in half.

In a large skillet combine 1 cup of the broth, the lemon peel, and black pepper. Bring to boiling; reduce heat. Carefully add the fish and asparagus. Cover and cook over medium-low heat for 4 minutes. Add yellow pepper. Cover and cook about 2 minutes more or until fish flakes easily with a fork. Using a slotted spatula, remove fish and vegetables; reserve liquid in skillet. Keep fish and vegetables warm.

For sauce, stir together the remaining broth and cornstarch. Stir into liquid in skillet. Cook and stir until thickened and bubbly. Cook and stir for 2 minutes more. Stir in chives. Arrange fish and vegetables on hot couscous or rice; top with sauce. Makes 4 servings.

Nutrition information per serving: 249 calories, 28 g protein, 29 g carbohydrate, 2 g fat (0 g saturated), 60 mg cholesterol, 390 mg sodium.

THAWING FISH

To thaw fish, place the unopened package in a container in the refrigerator and allow overnight thawing for a 1-pound package. If necessary, you can place the wrapped package of fish under cold running water for 1 to 2 minutes to hasten thawing. Thawing fish at room temperature or in warm water isn't recommended, since the fish won't thaw evenly and may spoil. Do not refreeze fish.

Pesto Sole Roll-Ups

Walleyed pike is often called the "sole" of fresh waters and has long been a favorite of fishermen. It works equally as well as sole or flounder in these carrot and pesto filled bundles.

4   4-ounce fresh or frozen sole or
      flounder fillets, ¼ to ½ inch thick
⅔   cup refrigerated pesto sauce
1   medium carrot, shredded (½ cup)
1   tablespoon margarine or butter,
      melted
3   tablespoons fine dry bread crumbs
1   teaspoon finely shredded lemon peel
6   ounces hot cooked fettuccine
1   tablespoon lemon juice
      Lemon wedges (optional)
      Carrot curls (optional)
      Fresh basil sprigs (optional)

Thaw fish, if frozen. Rinse fish; pat dry with paper towels. Spread one side of each fillet with about 1 tablespoon of the pesto. Sprinkle each fillet with 2 tablespoons of the shredded carrot. Starting from a short end, roll up fish around the carrot. Place fish rolls, seam sides down, in a 2-quart square baking dish. Brush fish rolls with melted margarine or butter.

Toss together bread crumbs and lemon peel; sprinkle over fish rolls. Bake, uncovered, in a 375° oven for 20 to 25 minutes or until fish flakes easily with a fork.

Toss together the remaining pesto, hot pasta, and lemon juice. Divide the pasta mixture evenly among dinner plates and top each with a fish roll. If desired, garnish with lemon wedges, carrot curls, and basil sprigs. Makes 4 servings.

Nutrition information per serving: 607 calories, 31 g protein, 47 g carbohydrate, 32 g fat (1 g saturated), 59 mg cholesterol, 475 mg sodium.

Sooner is Better

For best results, purchase fresh fish the same day you plan to cook it. When that's not possible, wrap the fish loosely in clear plastic wrap, store it in the coldest part of the refrigerator, and use it within 2 days. If you purchase frozen fish, keep it in a freezer set at 0° or lower for up to 3 months.

Halibut with Creamy Dijon Sauce

Feel like having a barbecue instead of cooking these fish steaks indoors? Grill the fish on a greased rack of an uncovered grill directly over medium coals for 8 to 12 minutes or until fish is done, turning fish and brushing once with the basting sauce.

---

4 fresh or frozen halibut or sea bass steaks, cut 1 inch thick (about 1½ pounds)
1 tablespoon margarine or butter, melted
¼ teaspoon onion salt
¼ teaspoon dried marjoram, crushed
¼ teaspoon dried thyme, crushed
½ cup dairy sour cream
1 tablespoon all-purpose flour
1 tablespoon Dijon-style mustard
⅛ teaspoon salt
⅛ teaspoon pepper
⅛ teaspoon dried thyme, crushed
½ cup chicken or vegetable broth
4 cups shredded spinach (5 ounces)
1 medium carrot, shredded (½ cup)
Lemon wedges (optional)

Thaw fish, if frozen. Rinse fish; pat dry with paper towels. Set aside.

For basting sauce, combine margarine or butter, onion salt, marjoram, and ¼ teaspoon thyme.

Place fish steaks on the rack of an unheated broiler pan. Brush with basting sauce. Broil 4 inches from the heat for 8 to 12 minutes or until fish flakes easily with a fork, turning and brushing once with the remaining basting sauce halfway through broiling.

Meanwhile, for Dijon sauce, in a small saucepan stir together the sour cream, flour, mustard, salt, pepper, and ⅛ teaspoon thyme. Add chicken or vegetable broth, stirring until well mixed. Cook and stir over medium heat until thickened and bubbly. Cook and stir for 1 minute more. Keep warm.

Toss together spinach and carrot. Line dinner plates with the spinach mixture. Arrange fish on spinach mixture. Top with Dijon sauce. If desired, garnish with lemon wedges. Makes 4 servings.

Nutrition information per serving: 282 calories, 39 g protein, 9 g carbohydrate, 9 g fat (2 g saturated), 59 mg cholesterol, 549 mg sodium.

Salmon with Wilted Greens

This dinner packs in all the vitamin C and almost half of the vitamin A you need for an entire day—all for under 300 calories.

4 fresh or frozen salmon steaks, cut
    ¾ inch thick (about 1 pound)
3 tablespoons orange juice concentrate
3 tablespoons water
2 tablespoons reduced-sodium
    soy sauce
1 tablespoon honey
2 teaspoons cooking oil
1 teaspoon toasted sesame oil
½ teaspoon grated gingerroot or
    ¼ teaspoon ground ginger
6 cups torn mixed greens (such as
    spinach, Swiss chard, radicchio, or
    mustard, beet, or collard greens)
1 small red sweet pepper, cut into
    thin strips
1 medium orange, peeled and
    sectioned
    Orange peel strips (optional)

Thaw fish, if frozen. For dressing, in a small bowl combine orange juice concentrate, water, soy sauce, honey, cooking oil, toasted sesame oil, and ginger.

Rinse fish; pat dry with paper towels. Place the fish on the greased unheated rack of a broiler pan. Broil 4 inches from the heat for 3 minutes. Using a wide spatula, carefully turn fish. Brush with 1 tablespoon of the dressing. Broil for 3 to 6 minutes more or until fish flakes easily with a fork.

(Or, grill fish on the greased rack of an uncovered grill directly over medium coals for 3 minutes. Carefully turn fish. Brush with 1 tablespoon of the dressing. Grill for 3 to 6 minutes more.)

Remove fish. Cover and keep warm. Place the greens in a large salad bowl. In a large skillet bring the remaining dressing to boiling. Add red pepper strips. Remove from heat. Pour over greens, tossing to coat.

To serve, divide greens mixture among dinner plates. Arrange the orange sections and fish on top of greens. If desired, garnish with orange peel strips. Serve immediately. Makes 4 servings.

Nutrition information per serving: 255 calories, 27 g protein, 15 g carbohydrate, 9 g fat (2 g saturated), 31 mg cholesterol, 406 mg sodium.

Shark and Shrimp with Broccoli

Shark, marlin, and swordfish are excellent choices for stir-frying because of their firm texture.

8 ounces fresh or frozen shark, marlin, or swordfish steaks, cut 1 inch thick

8 ounces fresh or frozen, peeled, deveined medium shrimp

2 tablespoons soy sauce

2 tablespoons dry sherry

1 teaspoon grated gingerroot

¾ teaspoon sugar

1 tablespoon cooking oil

1 clove garlic, minced

4 cups broccoli flowerets

1 medium red or green sweet pepper, chopped

2 cups hot cooked Chinese egg noodles or fine noodles

Thaw fish and shrimp, if frozen. Rinse fish and shrimp; pat dry with paper towels. Cut fish into 1-inch cubes. Discard any skin and bones.

In a medium bowl stir together fish, shrimp, soy sauce, sherry, gingerroot, and sugar. Cover and marinate in the refrigerator for 30 minutes. Drain fish and shrimp, reserving marinade. Set aside.

Add cooking oil to a wok or large skillet. Preheat over medium-high heat (add more oil if necessary during cooking). Stir-fry garlic in hot oil for 15 seconds. Add broccoli; stir-fry for 3 minutes. Add sweet pepper; stir-fry about 1 minute more or until vegetables are crisp-tender. Remove vegetables from wok.

Add half of the fish and shrimp to wok. Stir-fry for 3 to 5 minutes or until fish flakes easily with a fork, being careful not to break up pieces. Remove from wok. Repeat with the remaining fish and shrimp. Return all of the fish and shrimp to wok. Push fish and shrimp from center of wok.

Add marinade to center of wok. Cook and stir until bubbly. Return cooked vegetables to wok. Gently stir all ingredients together to coat. Cook and stir for 1 to 2 minutes more or until heated through. Serve immediately over hot noodles. Makes 4 servings.

Nutrition information per serving: 298 calories, 28 g protein, 28 g carbohydrate, 8 g fat (2 g saturated fat), 136 mg cholesterol, 695 mg sodium.

Nutty Parmesan Fish

A light and crispy coating that features cracker crumbs, pine nuts, and Parmesan cheese makes a flavor-packed breading for these oven-fried fish sticks.

1 pound fresh or frozen orange
   roughy or haddock fillets
1 beaten egg
2 tablespoons milk
¼ cup finely crushed rich round
   crackers
2 tablespoons grated Parmesan cheese
2 tablespoons ground pine nuts or
   almonds
½ teaspoon dried basil, crushed
⅛ teaspoon pepper
2 tablespoons margarine or butter,
   melted
   Tartar Sauce (optional)

Thaw fish, if frozen. Rinse fish; pat dry with paper towels. Cut fish into 1-inch-wide strips. Set aside.

In a shallow dish combine egg and milk. In another shallow dish combine cracker crumbs, Parmesan cheese, ground nuts, basil, and pepper. Dip fish pieces into egg mixture and then roll in crumb mixture. Place coated fish in a greased shallow baking pan. Drizzle melted margarine or butter over fish.

Bake in a 500° oven until coating is golden and fish flakes easily with a fork (allow 4 to 6 minutes per ½-inch thickness). If desired, serve with Tartar Sauce. Makes 4 servings.

Tartar Sauce: In a small bowl stir together 1 cup *mayonnaise* or *salad dressing*, ¼ cup finely chopped *dill pickle* or *sweet pickle relish*, 1 tablespoon sliced *green onion*, 1 tablespoon snipped *parsley*, 1 tablespoon diced *pimiento*, and 1 teaspoon *lemon juice*. Cover and chill until serving time. Makes about 1 cup.

Nutrition information per serving: 221 calories, 22 g protein, 5 g carbohydrate, 13 g fat (3 g saturated), 80 mg cholesterol, 267 mg sodium.

SHOPPING FOR FISH FILLETS

Trust your eyes and nose when buying fish fillets. Look for firm, moist, clean-cut fillets. Avoid those that have a strong or fishy odor and ragged edges.

Deep-Dish Tuna Pie

A convenient, off-the-shelf piecrust mix makes a flaky top that looks and tastes like you made it from scratch.

½ of an 11-ounce package piecrust mix (1⅓ cups)

1 large onion, chopped (1 cup)

1 medium potato, peeled and chopped (about 1 cup)

1 10¾-ounce can condensed cream of mushroom soup

⅓ cup grated Parmesan cheese

⅓ cup milk

1 tablespoon lemon juice

¾ teaspoon dried dillweed

¼ teaspoon pepper

1 16-ounce package frozen mixed vegetables

1 9¼-ounce can tuna, drained and broken into chunks

1 beaten egg

Prepare piecrust mix according to package directions, except do not roll out. Cover dough; set aside.

In a covered large skillet cook onion and potato in a small amount of boiling water about 7 minutes or until tender. Drain. Stir in soup, Parmesan cheese, milk, lemon juice, dillweed, and pepper. Cook and stir until mixture is bubbly. Gently stir in the frozen mixed vegetables and tuna. Spoon mixture into an ungreased 2-quart round casserole.

On a lightly floured surface, roll pastry into a circle 2 inches larger than the diameter of the top of the casserole and about ⅛ inch thick. Make 1-inch slits near the center of the pastry. Center pastry over top of casserole, allowing ends to hang over edge. Trim pastry ½ inch beyond edge of casserole. Turn pastry under; flute to the casserole edge, pressing gently. Brush pastry with beaten egg.

Bake in a 400° oven for 40 to 45 minutes or until crust is golden brown. Serve immediately. Makes 6 servings.

Nutrition information per serving: 386 calories, 21 g protein, 35 g carbohydrate, 18 g fat (5 g saturated), 49 mg cholesterol, 893 mg sodium.

CHOPPED ONIONS THE EASY WAY

To chop onions quickly, first cut the onion in half. Use the cut side as a base to stabilize the piece. Slice the onion half in one direction; holding the slices together with one hand, slice in the other direction. The job is easier if you use a chef's knife because it's designed to let you grasp the handle without your fingers touching the cutting surface.

Seafood Enchiladas

Imitation seafood is made commercially by processing and re-forming minced fish to look like shellfish. It's less expensive than crab or lobster and, as an added bonus, is lower in cholesterol.

8   6-inch corn tortillas
1   medium red onion, finely chopped
      (½ cup)
2   cloves garlic, minced
1   teaspoon ground coriander
¼   teaspoon black pepper
2   tablespoons margarine or butter
3   tablespoons all-purpose flour
1   8-ounce carton dairy sour cream
1   14½-ounce can chicken broth
1   or 2 canned jalapeño peppers,
      rinsed, seeded, and chopped, or
      one 4-ounce can diced green chile
      peppers, drained
1   cup shredded Monterey Jack cheese
      (4 ounces)
12 ounces flake-style imitation
      crabmeat
      Chopped tomatoes (optional)
      Cilantro sprigs (optional)

Wrap corn tortillas in foil. Heat in a 350° oven for 10 to 15 minutes or until softened.

Meanwhile, for sauce, in a medium saucepan cook the onion, garlic, coriander, and black pepper in margarine or butter over medium heat until onion is tender. In a medium bowl stir flour into sour cream; stir in broth. Add the sour cream mixture to onion mixture. Stir in jalapeño or green chile peppers. Cook and stir until mixture is slightly thickened and bubbly. Remove from heat. Add half of the cheese, stirring until melted.

For filling, stir ½ cup of the sauce into crabmeat. Place about ¼ cup of the filling on each tortilla; roll up. Arrange tortilla rolls, seam sides down, in a lightly greased 2-quart rectangular baking dish. Top with the remaining sauce. Bake, covered, in a 350° oven for 30 to 35 minutes or until heated through.

Sprinkle with the remaining cheese. Bake, uncovered, about 5 minutes more or until cheese is melted. Let stand for 10 minutes before serving. If desired, garnish with tomatoes, cilantro, and additional finely chopped red onion. Makes 4 servings.

Nutrition information per serving: 550 calories, 26 g protein, 44 g carbohydrate, 30 g fat (15 g saturated), 68 mg cholesterol, 1,461 mg sodium.

Shrimp Curry

Tease your taste buds with this invigorating alliance of sweet raisins and hot pepper sauce.

12 ounces fresh or frozen, peeled, deveined shrimp
1 large onion, chopped (1 cup)
1 medium green sweet pepper, cut into 1-inch pieces (1 cup)
1 stalk celery, sliced (½ cup)
1 clove garlic, minced
2 tablespoons cooking oil
1 14½-ounce can tomatoes, cut up
½ cup slivered almonds
½ cup raisins
¼ cup snipped parsley
¼ cup chili sauce
1 teaspoon lemon juice
½ teaspoon salt
½ teaspoon bottled hot pepper sauce
¼ teaspoon white pepper
¼ teaspoon curry powder
¼ teaspoon dried thyme, crushed
2 cups hot cooked rice
¼ cup slivered almonds, toasted

Thaw shrimp, if frozen. Rinse the shrimp; pat dry with paper towels. Set aside.

In a 12-inch skillet cook onion, green pepper, celery, and garlic in hot oil until crisp-tender. Stir in undrained tomatoes, ½ cup almonds, raisins, parsley, chili sauce, lemon juice, salt, hot pepper sauce, white pepper, curry powder, and thyme. Bring to boiling; reduce heat. Cover and simmer for 30 minutes.

Stir shrimp into tomato mixture. Return to boiling; reduce heat. Cover and simmer about 5 minutes more or until shrimp turn pink. Serve over rice. Sprinkle each serving with toasted almonds. Makes 4 servings.

Nutrition information per serving: 511 calories, 24 g protein, 63 g carbohydrate, 20 g fat (2 g saturated), 131 mg cholesterol, 841 mg sodium.

PEELING AND DEVEINING SHRIMP

To peel and devein shrimp, first open the shell of each shrimp lengthwise down the body. Start at the head and peel away the shell. Gently pull on the tail to remove it. Using a sharp knife, make a shallow slit along the back from the head to the tail. Locate the black vein. If the vein is exposed, hold the shrimp under cold running water; rinse away the vein. If it isn't, remove vein using the tip of a knife, then rinse.

Spicy Shrimp on Skewers

For a tangy accompaniment to the peppery shrimp, add fresh pineapple wedges to the grill alongside the shrimp during the last 5 minutes of grilling.

1½ pounds fresh or frozen large shrimp in shells
½ cup frozen pineapple juice concentrate, thawed
1 to 2 tablespoons finely chopped jalapeño peppers
1 teaspoon grated gingerroot or ⅛ teaspoon ground ginger
1 clove garlic, minced
¼ teaspoon crushed red pepper
   Hot cooked rice pilaf (optional)

Thaw shrimp, if frozen. Peel and devein shrimp. Rinse shrimp; pat dry with paper towels. Place shrimp in a plastic bag and set the bag into a shallow dish.

For marinade, in a small mixing bowl combine the pineapple juice concentrate, jalapeño peppers, ginger, garlic, and crushed red pepper. Pour over shrimp; seal bag. Marinate in the refrigerator for 1 to 2 hours, turning bag once.

Drain the shrimp, reserving marinade. Thread shrimp onto 5 long metal skewers.

Grill kabobs on an uncovered grill directly over medium coals for 6 to 8 minutes or until shrimp turn pink, turning and brushing once with marinade halfway through grilling.

(Or, in a covered grill arrange medium-hot coals around a drip pan. Test for medium heat above the pan. Place kabobs on grill rack over drip pan. Cover and grill for 8 to 10 minutes, brushing occasionally with marinade during the first half of grilling.)

If desired, serve the shrimp kabobs over hot cooked rice pilaf. Makes 5 servings.

Nutrition information per serving: 133 calories, 17 g protein, 13 g carbohydrate, 1 g fat (0 g saturated), 157 mg cholesterol, 181 mg sodium.

Fettuccine with Herbed Shrimp

A white wine and herb sauce dresses the shrimp and pasta in this elegant entrée.

12 ounces fresh or frozen, peeled, deveined shrimp
6 ounces packaged dried plain and/or spinach fettuccine
2 cups sliced fresh mushrooms
1 large onion, chopped (1 cup)
2 cloves garlic, minced
1 tablespoon olive oil or cooking oil
¼ cup dry white wine
1 tablespoon instant chicken bouillon granules
1 tablespoon snipped fresh basil or 1 teaspoon dried basil, crushed
1½ teaspoons snipped fresh oregano or ½ teaspoon dried oregano, crushed
1 teaspoon cornstarch
⅛ teaspoon pepper
2 medium tomatoes, peeled, seeded, and chopped
¼ cup grated Parmesan cheese
¼ cup snipped parsley

Thaw shrimp, if frozen. Rinse shrimp; pat dry with paper towels. Cut shrimp in half lengthwise; set aside.

Cook pasta according to package directions. Drain; keep warm.

Meanwhile, in a large saucepan cook mushrooms, onion, and garlic in hot oil until onion is tender.

In a small mixing bowl stir together wine, bouillon granules, basil, oregano, cornstarch, and pepper. Add to mushroom mixture. Cook and stir until thickened and bubbly.

Add shrimp to mushroom mixture. Cover and simmer about 2 minutes or until shrimp turn pink. Stir in tomatoes; heat through.

Spoon the shrimp mixture over pasta. Sprinkle with Parmesan cheese and parsley. Toss to coat. Makes 4 servings.

Nutrition information per serving: 351 calories, 25 g protein, 44 g carbohydrate, 7 g fat (2 g saturated), 136 mg cholesterol, 926 mg sodium.

SELECTING SHRIMP

At fish markets or supermarket fish counters, shrimp is usually sold by the pound. The price per pound is determined by size—the bigger the shrimp, the higher the price and the fewer per pound. Select fresh shrimp that are moist and firm, have translucent flesh, and smell fresh. Signs of poor quality are an unpleasant ammonia odor and blackened edges or spots on the shells.

Scallops in Curry Sauce

Because of their larger size, sea scallops work better than bay scallops for stir-frying. Choose scallops that are firm, sweet smelling, and free of excess cloudy liquid.

12 ounces fresh or frozen sea scallops
1 cup water
1 tablespoon cornstarch
2 teaspoons soy sauce
1 teaspoon sugar
1 tablespoon cooking oil
2 teaspoons grated gingerroot
4 cloves garlic, minced
3 stalks celery, thinly bias-sliced
2 medium carrots, thinly bias-sliced
4 ounces fresh mushrooms, quartered
      (1½ cups)
4 green onions, cut into 1-inch
      pieces (⅔ cup)
1 teaspoon curry powder
2 cups hot cooked rice
⅓ cup chutney
   Toasted Pita Wedges (see recipe,
      page 15) (optional)

Thaw scallops, if frozen. Rinse scallops; pat dry with paper towels. Cut any large scallops in half. Set aside.

For sauce, in a small bowl stir together the water, cornstarch, soy sauce, and sugar. Set aside.

Add cooking oil to a wok or large skillet. Preheat over medium-high heat (add more oil if necessary during cooking). Stir-fry the gingerroot and garlic in hot oil for 15 seconds. Add celery and carrots; stir-fry for 2 minutes. Add mushrooms and green onions; stir-fry for 1 minute. Sprinkle curry powder over vegetables. Stir-fry about 1 minute more or until vegetables are crisp-tender. Remove vegetables from wok.

Add scallops to wok. Stir-fry about 2 minutes or until scallops are opaque. Push scallops from center of wok.

Stir sauce; add to center of wok. Cook and stir until thickened and bubbly. Return cooked vegetables to wok. Gently stir all ingredients together to coat. Cook and stir for 1 to 2 minutes more or until heated through.

Serve immediately with hot cooked rice, chutney, and, if desired, Toasted Pita Wedges. Makes 4 servings.

Nutrition information per serving: 290 calories, 15 g protein, 48 g carbohydrate, 5 g fat (1 g saturated fat), 25 mg cholesterol, 359 mg sodium.

HERBED PASTA PRIMAVERA
(recipe, page 143)

Meatless
DISHES

Contents

Four Bean Enchiladas

We chose kidney, garbanzo, pinto, and navy or Great Northern beans to make this tasty crowd-size recipe, but you can use any combination of beans that you like.

16 6-inch corn tortillas
1 15-ounce can red kidney beans, rinsed and drained
1 15-ounce can garbanzo beans, rinsed and drained
1 15-ounce can pinto beans, rinsed and drained
1 15-ounce can navy or Great Northern beans, rinsed and drained
1 11-ounce can condensed cheddar cheese or nacho cheese soup
1 10-ounce can enchilada sauce
1 8-ounce can tomato sauce
1½ cups shredded Monterey Jack or cheddar cheese (6 ounces)
   Sliced pitted ripe olives (optional)
   Green sweet pepper strips (optional)

Wrap corn tortillas in foil and bake in a 350° oven about 10 minutes or until tortillas are warm.

For filling, in a large mixing bowl combine beans and cheese soup. Spoon about ⅓ cup filling onto one end of each tortilla. Starting from the end with the filling, roll up each tortilla.

Arrange tortillas, seam sides down, in 2 ungreased 2-quart rectangular baking dishes or 8 individual au gratin dishes.

In a medium mixing bowl stir together the enchilada sauce and tomato sauce. Pour over tortillas.

Cover and bake in the 350° oven about 30 minutes for baking dishes (about 20 minutes for au gratin dishes) or until heated through. Sprinkle with shredded cheese.

Bake, uncovered, about 5 minutes more or until cheese is melted. If desired, sprinkle the enchiladas with ripe olives and green pepper strips. Makes 8 servings.

Nutrition information per serving: 491 calories, 25 g protein, 71 g carbohydrate, 14 g fat (7 g saturated), 29 mg cholesterol, 1,599 mg sodium.

Savory Shepherd's Pie

To speed preparation, substitute packaged instant mashed potatoes (enough for 4 servings) for the 3 small potatoes and stir the garlic mixture into the prepared instant potatoes.

3	small potatoes (12 ounces)
2	cloves garlic, minced
½	teaspoon dried basil, crushed
2	tablespoons margarine or butter
¼	teaspoon salt
2	to 4 tablespoons milk
1	medium onion, chopped
1	medium carrot, sliced
1	tablespoon cooking oil
1	15-ounce can kidney beans, rinsed and drained
1	14½-ounce can tomatoes, drained and cut up
1	10-ounce package frozen mixed vegetables or whole kernel corn
1	8-ounce can tomato sauce
1	teaspoon Worcestershire sauce
½	teaspoon sugar
1	cup shredded cheddar cheese Paprika (optional)

Peel and quarter potatoes. In a covered large saucepan cook potatoes in a small amount of boiling, lightly salted water for 20 to 25 minutes or until tender. Drain.

Mash with a potato masher or beat with an electric mixer on low speed. In a small saucepan cook garlic and basil in margarine or butter for 15 seconds. Add to mashed potatoes along with salt. Gradually beat in enough of the milk to make light and fluffy. Set aside.

For filling, in a medium saucepan cook onion and carrot in hot oil until onion is tender. Stir in beans, tomatoes, frozen vegetables, tomato sauce, Worcestershire sauce, and sugar. Heat until mixture is bubbly.

Transfer filling to an ungreased 8x8x2-inch baking pan. Drop mashed potatoes in 4 mounds over filling. Sprinkle with cheddar cheese and, if desired, paprika. Bake in a 375° oven for 25 to 30 minutes or until heated through and cheese starts to brown. Makes 4 servings.

Nutrition information per serving: 456 calories, 20 g protein, 60 g carbohydrate, 19 g fat (8 g saturated), 31 mg cholesterol, 1,130 mg sodium.

Herbed Pasta Primavera

For the best flavor, use fresh parsley, fresh basil, and freshly shredded Parmesan cheese.

6 ounces packaged dried linguine, spaghetti, or fettuccine
1 cup water
2 teaspoons cornstarch
2 teaspoons instant vegetable or chicken bouillon granules
1 tablespoon olive oil
2 cloves garlic, minced
8 ounces asparagus, cut into 1-inch pieces
2 medium carrots, thinly bias-sliced
1 medium onion, chopped
1 6-ounce package frozen pea pods, thawed and well drained
⅔ cup sliced almonds
¼ cup snipped parsley
1½ teaspoons dried basil, crushed
¼ teaspoon pepper
⅓ cup finely shredded Parmesan cheese

Cook pasta according to package directions. Drain; keep warm. Meanwhile, for sauce, in a small bowl stir together the water, cornstarch, and vegetable or chicken bouillon granules. Set aside.

Add olive oil to a wok or large skillet. Preheat over medium-high heat. Stir-fry garlic in hot oil for 15 seconds. Add asparagus, carrots, and onion; stir fry for 2 minutes. Add pea pods, nuts, parsley, basil, and pepper. Stir-fry about 1 minute more or until vegetables are crisp-tender. Remove vegetable mixture from wok.

Stir sauce; add to wok. Cook and stir until thickened and bubbly. Cook and stir for 1 minute more. Return vegetable mixture to wok. Cook and stir until heated through. Serve immediately over pasta. Sprinkle with Parmesan cheese. Makes 4 servings.

Nutrition information per serving: 432 calories, 17 g protein, 52 g carbohydrate, 19 g fat (3 g saturated), 7 mg cholesterol, 642 mg sodium.

Vegetable Lasagna

In a hurry? Substitute 2 cups of prepared spaghetti sauce for the Red Pepper Sauce in this recipe.

6 no-boil lasagna noodles or regular
   lasagna noodles
8 ounces zucchini and/or yellow
   summer squash, halved
   lengthwise and sliced
2 cups sliced fresh mushrooms
⅓ cup chopped onion
2 teaspoons olive oil
1 cup fat-free or low-fat ricotta cheese
¼ cup finely shredded Parmesan cheese
¼ teaspoon black pepper
   Red Pepper Sauce
1 cup shredded part-skim mozzarella
   cheese (4 ounces)
1 medium tomato, seeded and
   chopped
   Fresh oregano sprigs (optional)

Soak the no-boil lasagna noodles in warm water for 10 minutes. (Or, cook regular noodles according to package directions, except omit salt.) Drain.

Meanwhile, in a large skillet cook zucchini and/or yellow squash, mushrooms, and onion in hot olive oil about 6 minutes or until squash is tender, stirring occasionally. Drain well.

In a small bowl stir together ricotta cheese, Parmesan cheese, and black pepper. To assemble, place 3 lasagna noodles in a 2-quart square baking dish, trimming to fit as necessary. Top with ricotta mixture, half of the vegetable mixture, half of the Red Pepper Sauce, and half of the mozzarella cheese. Layer with the remaining lasagna noodles, vegetable mixture, and sauce.

Bake in a 375° oven for 30 minutes. Sprinkle with remaining mozzarella cheese and the tomato. Bake about 5 minutes more or until heated through. Let stand for 10 minutes before serving. If desired, garnish with oregano sprigs. Makes 6 servings.

Red Pepper Sauce: In a large skillet cook 3 cups chopped *red sweet pepper* and 4 whole cloves *garlic* in 1 tablespoon *olive oil* or *cooking oil* over medium heat for 20 minutes, stirring occasionally. (Or, use one 12-ounce jar *roasted red sweet peppers*, drained. Omit cooking step.) Place mixture in a blender container. Cover and blend until nearly smooth. Add ½ cup *water,* ¼ cup *tomato paste,* 2 tablespoons *red wine vinegar,* and 1 tablespoon snipped *fresh oregano* or ½ teaspoon *dried oregano,* crushed. Cover and blend just until nearly smooth. Return to skillet; heat through. Makes 2 cups.

Nutrition information per serving: 249 calories, 17 g protein, 28 g carbohydrate, 9 g fat (3 g saturated), 18 mg cholesterol, 292 mg sodium.

Pasta Rosa-Verde

This red, white, and green dish on the table will make any flag-waving Italian feel patriotic (not to mention famished)! Fresh tomatoes are quick-cooked with peppery arugula and topped with tangy Gorgonzola cheese.

8 ounces packaged dried cut ziti or mostaccioli
1 medium onion, thinly sliced
2 cloves garlic, minced
1 tablespoon olive oil
4 to 6 medium tomatoes, seeded and coarsely chopped
1 teaspoon salt
½ teaspoon freshly ground black pepper
¼ teaspoon crushed red pepper (optional)
3 cups arugula, watercress, and/or spinach, coarsely chopped
¼ cup pine nuts or slivered almonds, toasted
2 tablespoons crumbled Gorgonzola or other blue cheese

Cook pasta according to package directions. Drain; keep warm.

Meanwhile, for sauce, in a large skillet cook the onion and garlic in hot olive oil over medium heat until onion is tender.

Add tomatoes, salt, black pepper, and, if desired, red pepper. Cook and stir over medium-high heat about 2 minutes or until the tomatoes are warm and release some of their juices. Stir in arugula, watercress, and/or spinach. Heat just until greens are wilted.

Arrange the pasta in individual serving bowls. Spoon the sauce over the pasta. Sprinkle with toasted pine nuts or almonds and Gorgonzola or other blue cheese. Makes 4 servings.

Nutrition information per serving: 352 calories, 12 g protein, 54 g carbohydrate, 11 g fat (2 g saturated), 3 mg cholesterol, 610 mg sodium.

ALL ABOUT ARUGULA

Arugula, sometimes called rocket, is a peppery, pungent salad green that adds a spicy flavor to dishes. Select arugula with fresh, small, rich green leaves. Avoid yellowed or wilted leaves. When you bring arugula home, refrigerate it in a plastic bag for up to 2 days. To use it, gently wash the leaves by immersing them in cold water until there is no trace of grit and sand. Pat the arugula leaves dry with paper towels.

Mu Shu Vegetable Roll-Ups

Instead of wrapping up our Mu Shu vegetables in the traditional Peking pancakes, we went Mexican and used ready-made flour tortillas. For easier handling, be sure to warm the tortillas before filling.

2 tablespoons water
2 tablespoons soy sauce
½ teaspoon sugar
½ teaspoon cornstarch
8 to 10 8-inch flour tortillas
1 tablespoon cooking oil
1 teaspoon grated gingerroot
2 cloves garlic, minced
2 medium carrots, cut into julienne strips
½ of a small head cabbage, shredded (3 cups)
1 medium zucchini, cut into julienne strips (1¼ cups)
4 cups sliced fresh mushrooms
2 cups fresh bean sprouts
½ of a medium jicama, peeled and cut into julienne strips (1 cup)
8 ounces firm tofu (bean curd), well drained and cut into ¾-inch cubes
8 green onions, sliced (1 cup)
¼ cup hoisin sauce
Cherry tomato flowers (optional)
Green onion brushes (optional)

For sauce, in a small bowl stir together water, soy sauce, sugar, and cornstarch. Set aside.

Wrap tortillas in foil and bake in a 350° oven about 10 minutes or until warm. [Or, just before serving, microwave tortillas, covered, on 100% power (high) about 1 minute or until warm.]

Meanwhile, pour cooking oil into a wok or large skillet. Preheat over medium-high heat (add more oil if necessary during cooking). Stir-fry gingerroot and garlic in hot oil for 15 seconds. Add carrot strips; stir-fry for 1 minute. Add cabbage and zucchini; stir-fry for 1 minute. Add mushrooms, bean sprouts, and jicama strips. Stir-fry for 1 to 2 minutes more or until vegetables are crisp-tender. Push vegetables from center of wok.

Stir sauce; add to center of wok. Cook and stir until thickened and bubbly. Add tofu and sliced green onions. Gently stir all ingredients together to coat. Cover and cook about 2 minutes more or until mixture is heated through.

Spread warm tortillas with hoisin sauce. Spoon the vegetable mixture onto each tortilla. Fold over one side of tortilla to cover some of the filling. Then fold the two adjacent sides of tortilla over filling. Secure with toothpicks, if necessary. If desired, garnish with tomato flowers and green onion brushes. Serve immediately. Makes 4 or 5 servings.

Nutrition information per serving: 399 calories, 20 g protein, 57 g carbohydrate, 12 g fat (2 g saturated fat), 0 mg cholesterol, 1,811 mg sodium.

South-of-the-Border Pie

Kidney beans, brown rice, eggs, and cheddar cheese provide the protein while chili powder and cumin provide the kick. Serve this Mexican-style dish with a simple tossed salad.

1 medium onion, chopped
2 cloves garlic, minced
1 tablespoon olive oil or cooking oil
1 to 2 teaspoons chili powder
1 teaspoon ground cumin
¼ teaspoon salt
1 15-ounce can red kidney beans, rinsed and drained
1½ cups cooked brown rice
1 cup shredded cheddar cheese (4 ounces)
¾ cup milk
2 slightly beaten eggs
Green sweet pepper strips (optional)
Salsa (optional)

Lightly grease a 10-inch quiche dish or pie plate. Set aside. In a large saucepan cook onion and garlic in hot oil until tender. Stir in chili powder, cumin, and salt. Cook and stir for 1 minute more. Cool. Stir in beans, cooked brown rice, cheese, milk, and eggs.

Spoon the bean mixture into the prepared baking dish. Bake in a 350° oven about 25 minutes or until the center is set. Let stand for 10 minutes. If desired, sprinkle the pie with green pepper strips and serve with salsa. Makes 6 servings.

Nutrition information per serving: 254 calories, 14 g protein, 26 g carbohydrate, 12 g fat (5 g saturated), 93 mg cholesterol, 366 mg sodium.

SODIUM SENSE FOR BEANS

Using canned beans in recipes can save you time, but they also can contribute sodium to your diet. A simple solution to this salty situation is to rinse the beans in a colander under running water and let them drain. You'll still have great tasting beans without the salty liquid that comes with them.

Southern Grits Casserole with Red Pepper Relish

To make a roasted pepper relish, substitute one 12-ounce jar roasted red sweet peppers for the fresh sweet peppers. Drain and chop the roasted peppers and stir into the cooked onion mixture.

4 cups water
1 cup quick-cooking grits
4 slightly beaten eggs
2 cups shredded cheddar cheese (8 ounces)
½ cup milk
¼ cup sliced green onions
1 to 2 jalapeño peppers, seeded (if desired) and chopped
½ teaspoon garlic salt
¼ teaspoon white pepper
  Sliced green onions (optional)
2 medium red sweet peppers, chopped (2 cups)
1 small red onion, chopped (½ cup)
2 cloves garlic, minced
1 tablespoon margarine or butter
⅓ cup snipped parsley
1 tablespoon white wine vinegar

In a large saucepan bring water to boiling. Slowly stir in grits. Gradually stir about 1 cup of the hot mixture into the eggs. Return to saucepan. Remove from heat.

Stir the shredded cheese, milk, ¼ cup green onions, jalapeño peppers, garlic salt, and white pepper into the grits mixture.

Spoon the grits mixture into an ungreased 2-quart casserole. Bake in a 350° oven for 45 to 50 minutes or until a knife inserted near center comes out clean If desired, sprinkle with additional green onions.

Meanwhile, for relish, in a medium saucepan cook the red sweet peppers, red onion, and garlic in margarine or butter just until peppers are tender. Remove from heat. Stir in parsley and vinegar.

Let relish stand at room temperature at least 30 minutes. Serve the relish with grits. Makes 4 servings.

Nutrition information per serving: 403 calories, 23 g protein, 16 g carbohydrate, 27 g fat (14 g saturated), 275 mg cholesterol, 731 mg sodium.

Vegetarian Fried Rice

Transform fried rice from a side dish into a sumptuous meal by adding extra eggs and lots of vegetables.

5 slightly beaten eggs
1 tablespoon soy sauce
2 tablespoons cooking oil
1 small onion, chopped (⅓ cup)
1 clove garlic, minced
2 stalks celery, thinly bias-sliced
   (1 cup)
1½ cups sliced fresh mushrooms
1 medium green sweet pepper,
   chopped (¾ cup)
4 cups cold cooked rice
1 8-ounce can bamboo shoots,
   drained
2 medium carrots, shredded (1 cup)
¾ cup frozen peas, thawed
3 tablespoons soy sauce
3 green onions, sliced (⅓ cup)
   Crinkle-cut carrot slices (optional)

In a small bowl combine eggs and 1 tablespoon soy sauce. Set aside.

Add 1 tablespoon of the cooking oil to a wok or large skillet. Preheat over medium heat. Stir-fry chopped onion and garlic in hot oil about 2 minutes or until crisp-tender.

Add the egg mixture to wok and stir gently to scramble. When eggs are set, remove from wok. Cut up any large pieces of egg mixture. Let wok cool slightly.

Add remaining oil to cooled wok. Preheat over medium-high heat (add more oil if necessary during cooking). Stir-fry celery in hot oil for 1 minute. Add the mushrooms and green pepper; stir-fry for 1 to 2 minutes more or until vegetables are crisp-tender.

Add cooked rice, bamboo shoots, shredded carrots, and peas. Sprinkle with 3 tablespoons soy sauce. Cook and stir for 4 to 6 minutes or until heated through. Add the cooked egg mixture and green onions. Cook and stir about 1 minute more or until heated through.

If desired, garnish fried rice with carrot slices. Serve immediately. Makes 4 or 5 servings.

Nutrition information per serving: 438 calories, 17 g protein, 61 g carbohydrate, 14 g fat (3 g saturated fat), 266 mg cholesterol, 1,177 mg sodium.

Fresh Tomato Pizza with Pesto

For best results, make this recipe when ripe, juicy summer tomatoes are at their peak.

½ cup pesto
1 12-inch Italian bread shell (Boboli)
3 medium ripe tomatoes, thinly sliced
1 2¼-ounce can sliced pitted ripe olives, drained (scant ⅔ cup)
Freshly ground pepper
2 cups shredded Monterey Jack or mozzarella cheese (8 ounces)

Spread pesto evenly over bread shell. Place on large pizza pan or baking sheet. Top with tomato slices. Sprinkle with olives and pepper. Top with Monterey Jack or mozzarella cheese.

Bake in a 425° oven for 10 to 15 minutes or until cheese is melted and tomatoes are warm. Cut into wedges. Makes 4 servings.

Nutrition information per serving: 776 calories, 32 g protein, 60 g carbohydrate, 48 g fat (11 g saturated), 60 mg cholesterol, 1,265 mg sodium.

Double Corn Tortilla Casserole

The double dose of corn comes from corn tortillas and whole kernel corn. Serve this tangy home-style dish with your favorite salsa or picante sauce.

8 6-inch corn tortillas
1½ cups shredded Monterey Jack cheese (6 ounces)
1 cup frozen whole kernel corn
4 green onions, sliced
2 slightly beaten eggs
1 cup buttermilk
1 4-ounce can diced green chile peppers

Grease a 2-quart square baking dish. Tear tortillas into bite-size pieces. Arrange half of the tortillas in prepared baking dish. Top with half of the cheese, half of the corn, and half of the green onions. Layer with the remaining tortillas, cheese, corn, and green onions.

In a medium mixing bowl stir together the eggs, buttermilk, and undrained chile peppers. Gently pour over tortilla mixture. Bake in a 325° oven about 30 minutes or until a knife inserted near the center comes out clean. Serve warm. Makes 4 servings.

Nutrition information per serving: 388 calories, 21 g protein, 37 g carbohydrate, 18 g fat (9 g saturated), 146 mg cholesterol, 564 mg sodium.

Fresh Tomato Pizza with Pesto

Spaghetti Squash Italiano

Spaghetti squash is a tasty, low-calorie, high-vitamin substitute for spaghetti.

2 small spaghetti squash (1¼ to 1½ pounds each)

4 ounces mozzarella cheese, cut into small cubes (1 cup)

3 medium tomatoes, seeded and chopped (2 cups)

4 green onions, sliced

½ cup pine nuts or coarsely chopped walnuts, toasted

¼ cup snipped fresh basil or parsley

1 tablespoon olive oil or cooking oil

2 cloves garlic, minced

2 tablespoons grated Parmesan cheese

Halve the squash lengthwise and remove the seeds. Prick skin all over with a sharp knife. Place halves, cut sides down, in a 3-quart rectangular baking dish. Cover and bake in a 350° oven for 60 to 70 minutes or until squash is tender.

Using a fork, carefully rake the squash pulp to separate it into strands, leaving the strands in the shells. Sprinkle one-fourth of the mozzarella cheese over each shell; toss lightly. Push the squash mixture up the sides of the shells.

Meanwhile, for filling, in a medium mixing bowl combine tomatoes, green onions, nuts, basil or parsley, oil, and garlic. Spoon the filling into squash shells. Sprinkle with Parmesan cheese.

Return to baking dish. Bake about 20 minutes more or until filling is heated through. Makes 4 servings.

Nutrition information per serving: 304 calories, 15 g protein, 23 g carbohydrate, 20 g fat (6 g saturated), 18 mg cholesterol, 237 mg sodium.

QUICK-COOKING SPAGHETTI SQUASH

Save time by cooking spaghetti squash in your microwave oven. Prick whole squash with a sharp knife. Place squash in a microwave-safe baking dish. Micro-cook, uncovered, on 100% power (high) for 15 to 20 minutes or until tender. Let stand for 5 minutes. Halve squash lengthwise and remove seeds.

Crispy Eggplant with Tomato-Feta Cheese Sauce

For a mild cheese flavor, sprinkle feta cheese over the spaghetti sauce. For a more robust cheese flavor, use blue cheese.

1   medium eggplant (about 1 pound), peeled and thinly sliced
2   slightly beaten eggs
2   tablespoons milk
½   cup grated Parmesan cheese
½   cup toasted wheat germ
1   teaspoon dried basil, crushed
¼   teaspoon black pepper
2   cups meatless spaghetti sauce
¼   to ½ teaspoon ground red pepper
1   cup crumbled feta or blue cheese
    Snipped fresh basil (optional)

Place eggplant slices on a baking sheet. Sprinkle lightly with salt. Let stand for 10 minutes. Pat eggplant dry with paper towels.

Grease a baking sheet. Set aside. In a shallow bowl combine the eggs and milk. In another shallow bowl stir together the Parmesan cheese, wheat germ, dried basil, and black pepper.

Dip the eggplant slices in egg mixture, then into wheat germ mixture, turning to coat both sides. Place the coated slices in a single layer on prepared baking sheet.

Bake in a 400° oven for 15 to 20 minutes or until the eggplant is crisp on outside and tender on inside.

Meanwhile, for sauce, in a medium saucepan combine the spaghetti sauce and ground red pepper. Cook over medium heat until mixture is heated through.

To serve, divide the eggplant slices among dinner plates. Spoon the sauce over eggplant. Sprinkle with feta or blue cheese and, if desired, snipped fresh basil. Makes 4 servings.

Nutrition information per serving: 388 calories, 20 g protein, 35 g carbohydrate, 20 g fat (9 g saturated), 142 mg cholesterol, 1,471 mg sodium.

Sautéed Onion & Tomato Sandwiches

When laps double as the dining table, the best TV dinner is something easy and out-of-hand. This hearty whole-grain sandwich serves perfectly. Pass around beer, brownies, and your biggest napkins.

2 medium onions, sliced
1 teaspoon olive oil
8 slices hearty whole grain bread
   (toasted, if desired)
   Honey mustard
4 lettuce leaves, shredded
3 small red and/or yellow tomatoes,
   thinly sliced
   Small fresh basil leaves
4 ounces spreadable Brie cheese or
   ½ of an 8-ounce tub cream cheese

In a large skillet cook the onion slices in hot olive oil over medium-high heat for 5 to 7 minutes or until tender and just starting to brown. Remove from heat. Cool onions slightly.

To assemble, lightly spread half of the bread slices with honey mustard. Top with shredded lettuce, cooked onion slices, and tomato slices. Sprinkle with basil leaves.

Spread the remaining bread slices with Brie or cream cheese. Place on top of sandwiches. Makes 4 servings.

Nutrition information per serving: 287 calories, 12 g protein, 35 g carbohydrate, 12 g fat (6 g saturated), 28 mg cholesterol, 490 mg sodium.

Cheese and Veggie Sandwiches

If you're watching your sodium intake, you can reduce the salt in the cottage cheese by placing it in a colander and rinsing under cold water.

1½ cups cottage cheese, drained
¼ cup shredded carrot
¼ cup chopped celery or green sweet
   pepper
½ teaspoon finely snipped fresh chives
¼ cup plain low-fat yogurt
8 small slices whole grain bread
2 tablespoons horseradish mustard
   Spinach or lettuce leaves
4 tomato slices

In a medium bowl combine the cottage cheese, carrot, celery or green pepper, and chives. Stir in the yogurt.

Spread the whole grain bread slices with horseradish mustard. Place the spinach or lettuce leaves on half of the bread slices. Top with the cottage cheese mixture, tomato slices, and the remaining bread slices. Makes 4 servings.

Nutrition information per serving: 232 calories, 16 g protein, 29 g carbohydrate, 7 g fat (3 g saturated), 13 mg cholesterol, 722 mg sodium.

Sautéed Onion & Tomato Sandwiches

Cookies
& CAKES

Contents

CITRUS-HAZELNUT BARS
(recipe, page 169)

White-Chocolate-Raspberry Cookies

If it's your turn to host the block party or the Christmas party, try these handsome melt-in-your-mouth cookies. They're elegant and sophisticated enough to serve as a simple dessert.

8	ounces white baking bars
½	cup butter
1	cup sugar
1	teaspoon baking soda
¼	teaspoon salt
2	eggs
2¾	cups all-purpose flour
½	cup seedless raspberry jam
3	ounces white baking bars
½	teaspoon shortening

Grease a cookie sheet. Set aside. Chop 4 ounces of the white baking bars. Set aside. In a heavy small saucepan heat another 4 ounces of the white baking bars over low heat until melted, stirring constantly. Cool.

In a large mixing bowl beat butter with an electric mixer on medium to high speed for 30 seconds. Add the sugar, baking soda, and salt; beat until combined. Beat in the eggs and melted white baking bars until combined. Beat in as much of the flour as you can with the mixer. Stir in any remaining flour with a wooden spoon. Stir in the 4 ounces chopped white baking bars.

Drop dough by a rounded teaspoon about 2 inches apart onto the prepared cookie sheet. Bake in a 375° oven for 7 to 9 minutes or until edges are lightly browned. Cool on cookie sheet for 1 minute. Transfer the cookies to a wire rack; cool.

Just before serving, in a small saucepan heat the raspberry jam over low heat until melted, stirring occasionally. Spoon about ½ teaspoon jam onto the top of each cookie.

In a heavy small saucepan combine the 3 ounces white baking bars and shortening. Heat over low heat until melted, stirring constantly. Drizzle over cookies. If necessary, chill about 15 minutes to firm baking bar mixture. Makes about 48 cookies.

Nutrition information per cookie: 104 calories, 1 g protein, 16 g carbohydrate, 4 g fat (2 g saturated), 14 mg cholesterol, 66 mg sodium.

Ultimate Bar Cookies

Crush any leftover bars and sprinkle over ice cream as a topping.

2 cups all-purpose flour
½ cup packed brown sugar
½ cup butter, softened
1 cup coarsely chopped walnuts
1 3½-ounce jar macadamia nuts, coarsely chopped (1 cup)
1 6-ounce package white baking bars, coarsely chopped (1 cup)
1 cup milk chocolate pieces
¾ cup butter
½ cup packed brown sugar

In a medium bowl beat flour, ½ cup brown sugar, and ½ cup butter with an electric mixer on medium speed until mixture forms fine crumbs. Press into the bottom of an ungreased 13x9x2-inch baking pan. Bake in a 350° oven about 15 minutes or until lightly browned.

Transfer pan to a wire rack. Sprinkle nuts, baking bars, and milk chocolate pieces over hot crust. Cook and stir ¾ cup butter and ½ cup brown sugar until bubbly. Cook and stir for 1 minute more. Pour over nuts and chocolate in pan. Bake about 15 minutes more or just until bubbly around edges. Cool in pan on a wire rack. Cut into desired shapes. Makes 36 bars.

Nutrition information per bar: 188 calories, 2 g protein, 16 g carbohydrate, 13 g fat (6 g saturated), 18 mg cholesterol, 12 mg sodium.

Mocha Brownies

These buttery mocha brownies boast plenty of semisweet chocolate and a delightful hint of tangerine.

⅔ cup butter
⅓ cup unsweetened cocoa powder
1 teaspoon instant coffee crystals
1 cup granulated sugar
2 eggs
1 teaspoon vanilla
¾ cup all-purpose flour
½ cup semisweet chocolate pieces or chopped semisweet chocolate
1 teaspoon finely shredded tangerine or orange peel
Powdered sugar (optional)

Grease an 8x8x2-inch baking pan. Set aside. In a medium saucepan melt butter. Stir in cocoa powder and coffee crystals. Remove from heat. Stir in the granulated sugar. Stir in eggs, one at a time, and vanilla. Beat lightly by hand just until combined. Stir in flour. Stir in chocolate pieces and shredded peel.

Spread into prepared pan. Bake in a 350° oven for 30 minutes. Cool in pan on a wire rack. If desired, sift powdered sugar over top. Cut into bars. Makes 24 brownies.

Nutrition information per brownie: 123 calories, 1 g protein, 13 g carbohydrate, 7 g fat (2 g saturated), 24 mg cholesterol, 52 mg sodium.

Citrus-Hazelnut Bars

Definitely a bar cookie with lots of appeal—these double citrus and nutty delights are not overly sweet and make a great accompaniment to an afternoon tea break.

⅓ cup butter
¼ cup granulated sugar
1 cup all-purpose flour
⅓ cup finely chopped hazelnuts
　　(filberts) or chopped almonds,
　　toasted
2 eggs
¾ cup granulated sugar
2 tablespoons all-purpose flour
1 teaspoon finely shredded orange
　　peel
2 tablespoons orange juice
1 teaspoon finely shredded lemon peel
1 tablespoon lemon juice
½ teaspoon baking powder
　　Powdered sugar (optional)

For crust, in a medium mixing bowl beat the butter with an electric mixer on medium to high speed for 30 seconds. Add the ¼ cup granulated sugar. Beat until thoroughly combined. Beat in the 1 cup flour and about half of the nuts until mixture is crumbly.

Press mixture onto bottom of an ungreased 8x8x2-inch baking pan. Bake in a 350° oven about 10 minutes or until lightly browned.

Meanwhile, in a medium mixing bowl combine eggs, the ¾ cup granulated sugar, the 2 tablespoons flour, orange peel, orange juice, lemon peel, lemon juice, and baking powder. Beat on medium speed about 2 minutes or until combined. Pour over hot crust. Sprinkle with the remaining nuts.

Bake about 20 minutes more or until light brown around the edges and center is set. Cool in pan on a wire rack. If desired, sift powdered sugar over top. Cut into bars. Store bars, covered, in the refrigerator. Makes 20 bars.

Nutrition information per bar: 111 calories, 2 g protein, 16 g carbohydrate, 5 g fat (1 g saturated), 25 mg cholesterol, 43 mg sodium.

Creamy, Fudgy, Nutty Brownies

The creamy crown on these brownies is essentially a chocolate cheesecake mixture, so store them in the refrigerator.

4	ounces unsweetened chocolate, chopped
½	cup butter
1	cup all-purpose flour
½	cup chopped walnuts or pecans, toasted
¼	teaspoon baking powder
1½	cups sugar
3	eggs
1	teaspoon vanilla
3	ounces semisweet chocolate, chopped
2	3-ounce packages cream cheese, softened
¼	cup sugar
1	egg
1	tablespoon milk
½	teaspoon vanilla

Grease and lightly flour an 8x8x2-inch baking pan. Set aside. In a small saucepan heat the unsweetened chocolate and butter until melted, stirring occasionally. Remove from heat. Cool slightly. In a medium bowl stir together flour, nuts, and baking powder. Set aside.

In a large mixing bowl stir together melted chocolate mixture and 1½ cups sugar. Add the 3 eggs and the 1 teaspoon vanilla. Using a wooden spoon, lightly beat mixture just until combined (don't overbeat or brownies will rise too high, then fall). Stir in flour mixture.

Spread the brownie batter in the prepared pan. Bake in a 350° oven for 40 minutes.

Meanwhile, for topping, in a heavy small saucepan heat the semisweet chocolate over low heat until melted, stirring constantly. Cool slightly. In a medium mixing bowl beat the melted semisweet chocolate, softened cream cheese, the ¼ cup sugar, 1 egg, milk, and ½ teaspoon vanilla until combined.

Carefully spread topping evenly over hot brownies. Bake about 10 minutes more or until topping appears set. Cool in pan on a wire rack. Cover and chill at least 2 hours before serving. Cut into bars. Store bars, covered, in the refrigerator. Makes 12 brownies.

Nutrition information per brownie: 409 calories, 7 g protein, 43 g carbohydrate, 27 g fat (9 g saturated), 97 mg cholesterol, 143 mg sodium.

Ultimate Bar Cookies (recipe, page 168) and
Creamy, Fudgy, Nutty Brownies

Cranberry-Pecan Tassies

Fruit- and nut-filled tassies—old Scottish for "little cups"—dress up the after-dinner plate with their special-occasion flavor and homestyle comfort.

½ cup butter, softened
1 3-ounce package cream cheese, softened
1 cup all-purpose flour
1 egg
¾ cup packed brown sugar
1 teaspoon vanilla
   Dash salt
⅓ cup finely chopped cranberries
3 tablespoons chopped pecans

For pastry, in a medium mixing bowl beat the butter and cream cheese with an electric mixer on medium to high speed until combined. Stir in the flour. If desired, chill the pastry for 1 hour.

Shape the pastry into 24 balls. Place pastry in ungreased 1¾-inch muffin cups. Press pastry evenly against the bottom and up the side of each muffin cup.

For filling, in another medium mixing bowl beat together the egg, brown sugar, vanilla, and salt just until smooth. Stir in the cranberries and pecans. Spoon the filling into the pastry-lined muffin cups.

Bake in a 325° oven for 30 to 35 minutes or until pastry is golden brown. Cool in muffin cups on wire racks. Remove tassies from muffin cups by running a knife around the edges. Makes 24 tassies.

Nutrition information per tassie: 94 calories, 1 g protein, 10 g carbohydrate, 6 g fat (3 g saturated), 23 mg cholesterol, 59 mg sodium.

STORING BAKED COOKIES

To store cookies after baking, cool completely; do not frost. In an airtight or freezer container, arrange cookies in a single layer; cover with a sheet of waxed paper. Repeat layers, leaving enough air space to close the container easily. Store at room temperature up to 3 days or freeze up to 8 months.

Oatmeal Cake

The natural goodness of rolled oats together with brown sugar and cinnamon give this old-fashioned cake its wonderful flavor.

1¼ cups boiling water
1 cup rolled oats
2 cups all-purpose flour
2 teaspoons baking powder
¾ teaspoon ground cinnamon
½ teaspoon baking soda
½ teaspoon salt
¼ teaspoon ground nutmeg
½ cup butter, softened
¾ cup granulated sugar
½ cup packed brown sugar
1 teaspoon vanilla
2 eggs
 Broiled Nut Topping

Grease and lightly flour a 9-inch springform pan. Set aside. Pour boiling water over oats; stir until combined. Let stand for 20 minutes. In a medium bowl combine the flour, baking powder, cinnamon, baking soda, salt, and nutmeg. Set aside.

In a large mixing bowl beat butter with an electric mixer on medium to high speed for 30 seconds. Add granulated sugar, brown sugar, and vanilla; beat until combined. Add eggs, one at a time, beating well after each. Alternately add flour mixture and oat mixture, beating on low to medium speed after each addition just until combined. Pour the batter into prepared pan.

Bake in a 350° oven for 40 to 45 minutes or until a wooden toothpick inserted near the center comes out clean. Cool in pan on a wire rack for 20 minutes. Remove side of pan; cool cake on rack at least 1 hour.

Transfer cake to a baking sheet. Spread Broiled Nut Topping over cake. Broil about 4 inches from the heat for 2 to 3 minutes or until topping is bubbly and golden brown. Cool on wire rack before serving. Makes 12 servings.

Broiled Nut Topping: In a saucepan combine ¼ cup *butter* and 2 tablespoons *half-and-half, light cream,* or *milk.* Cook and stir over medium heat until butter is melted. Add ½ cup packed *brown sugar;* stir until sugar is dissolved. Remove from heat. Stir in ¾ cup chopped *pecans* or *walnuts* and ⅓ cup flaked *coconut.*

Nutrition information per serving: 388 calories, 5 g protein, 52 g carbohydrate, 18 g fat (9 g saturated), 67 mg cholesterol, 296 mg sodium.

Upside-Down Pineapple-Orange Cake

For a twist on pineapple upside-down cake, we added mandarin oranges, using half a can of pineapple slices and half a can of orange sections. If you prefer to make the cake with just one fruit, use a whole can.

⅔ cup packed brown sugar
6 tablespoons butter
1½ teaspoons finely shredded orange peel
1 11-ounce can mandarin orange sections
1 8-ounce can pineapple slices
1⅓ cups all-purpose flour
1¼ teaspoons baking powder
½ teaspoon salt
6 tablespoons butter
1 cup granulated sugar
¼ teaspoon almond extract
2 eggs
⅔ cup dairy sour cream
    Sweetened Whipped Cream (optional)

In a saucepan combine brown sugar, 6 tablespoons butter, and orange peel. Cook and stir over medium heat until mixture is bubbly. Pour into an ungreased 9x9x2-inch baking pan.

Drain the oranges and pineapple. Cut half of the pineapple slices in half. Arrange the half slices of pineapple and half of the orange sections in pan. (Reserve remaining oranges and pineapple for another use.) Combine flour, baking powder, and salt.

In a large mixing bowl beat 6 tablespoons butter with an electric mixer on medium to high speed for 30 seconds. Add granulated sugar and almond extract; beat until combined. Add eggs, one at a time, beating well after each. Alternately add flour mixture and sour cream, beating on low to medium speed after each addition just until combined. Spoon over fruit.

Bake in a 350° oven for 35 to 40 minutes or until a wooden toothpick inserted near the center comes out clean. Cool in pan on a wire rack for 5 minutes. Invert onto a serving plate. Serve warm. If desired, top with Sweetened Whipped Cream. Makes 8 servings.

Sweetened Whipped Cream: In a chilled medium mixing bowl combine 1 cup *whipping cream*, 2 tablespoons *granulated sugar*, and ½ teaspoon *vanilla*. Beat with an electric mixer on medium to high speed until soft peaks form (tips curl).

Nutrition information per serving: 455 calories, 4 g protein, 64 g carbohydrate, 21 g fat (12 g saturated), 107 mg cholesterol, 371 mg sodium.

Banana Cake with Penuche Frosting

For a combination that's hard to beat, frost this easy-to-make cake right in the pan with the creamy brown sugar frosting.

2½ cups all-purpose flour
1½ cups granulated sugar
1½ teaspoons baking powder
1 teaspoon baking soda
½ teaspoon salt
1 cup mashed ripe bananas (about 3 bananas)
⅔ cup buttermilk or sour milk*
½ cup shortening
1 teaspoon vanilla
2 eggs
Penuche Frosting
Chopped nuts (optional)

Grease a 13x9x2-inch baking pan. Set aside. In a large mixing bowl combine flour, 1½ cups sugar, baking powder, baking soda, and salt. Add the bananas, buttermilk or sour milk, shortening, and vanilla.

Beat with an electric mixer on low speed until combined. Add eggs. Beat on medium speed for 2 minutes. Pour into the prepared pan.

Bake in a 350° oven about 35 minutes or until a wooden toothpick inserted near the center comes out clean. Cool completely in pan on a wire rack.

Frost with Penuche Frosting. If desired, immediately sprinkle with chopped nuts. Makes 12 to 16 servings.

*Note: To make ⅔ cup sour milk, place 2 teaspoons *lemon juice* or *vinegar* in a glass measuring cup. Add enough *milk* to make ⅔ cup total liquid; stir. Let stand for 5 minutes before using.

Penuche Frosting: In a medium saucepan melt ⅓ cup *butter* over medium heat. Stir in ⅔ cup packed *brown sugar.* Cook and stir until bubbly. Remove from heat. Add 3 tablespoons *milk,* beating vigorously until smooth. By hand, beat in enough sifted *powdered sugar* (about 2½ cups) to make a frosting of spreading consistency. Frost cake immediately.

Nutrition information per serving: 470 calories, 4 g protein, 82 g carbohydrate, 15 g fat (6 g saturated), 50 mg cholesterol, 274 mg sodium.

Busy-Day Cake

No time to bake? Stir up this one-bowl cake in only minutes with easy-to-keep-on-hand ingredients. Another time, skip the topping and serve it with fresh fruit and whipped cream.

1⅓ cups all-purpose flour
⅔ cup granulated sugar
2 teaspoons baking powder
⅔ cup milk
¼ cup butter, softened
1 egg
1 teaspoon vanilla
 Broiled Coconut Topping

Grease and flour an 8x1½-inch round baking pan. Set aside. In a large mixing bowl combine the flour, ⅔ cup sugar, and baking powder. Add the milk, butter, egg, and vanilla.

Beat with an electric mixer on low speed for 30 seconds. Beat on medium speed for 1 minute. Pour the batter into the prepared pan.

Bake in a 350° oven for 25 to 30 minutes or until a wooden toothpick inserted near the center comes out clean. Remove from heat.

Spread the Broiled Coconut Topping over the warm cake. Broil about 4 inches from the heat for 3 to 4 minutes or until topping is golden brown. Cool cake slightly in pan on a wire rack. Serve warm. Makes 8 servings.

Broiled Coconut Topping: In a medium mixing bowl stir together ¼ cup packed *brown sugar* and 2 tablespoons softened *butter*. Stir in 1 tablespoon *milk*. Stir in ½ cup flaked *coconut*, and, if desired, ¼ cup chopped *nuts*.

Nutrition information per serving: 281 calories, 4 g protein, 42 g carbohydrate, 11 g fat (6 g saturated), 51 mg cholesterol, 128 mg sodium.

Apple Cake

Generously rippled with apple slices and cinnamon and drizzled with powdered sugar icing, this luscious cake is especially welcome for breakfast or brunch on crisp autumn mornings.

¼ cup granulated sugar
2 tablespoons all-purpose flour
1½ teaspoons ground cinnamon
5 cups sliced, peeled cooking apples
2½ cups all-purpose flour
1½ cups granulated sugar
1½ teaspoons baking powder
½ teaspoon baking soda
1 cup cooking oil
4 eggs
¼ cup orange juice
2 teaspoons vanilla
   Powdered Sugar Icing

Grease and lightly flour a 10-inch fluted tube pan. Set aside. In a large mixing bowl combine ¼ cup sugar, 2 tablespoons flour, and cinnamon. Add apples; toss gently to coat. Set aside.

In another large mixing bowl combine 2½ cups flour, 1½ cups sugar, baking powder, and baking soda. Add oil, eggs, orange juice, and vanilla. Beat with an electric mixer on low to medium speed for 30 seconds. Beat on medium speed for 2 minutes.

Pour one-third of the batter (about 1½ cups) into the prepared pan. Top with half of the apple mixture. Spoon another one-third of the batter over apples in pan; top with the remaining apple mixture. Spoon the remaining batter over apples.

Bake in a 350° oven about 1¼ hours or until a wooden toothpick inserted near the center comes out clean.

Cool in pan on a wire rack for 15 minutes. Remove from pan. Cool completely on wire rack. Drizzle with Powdered Sugar Icing. Let cake stand for 1 to 2 hours before slicing. Makes 16 servings.

Powdered Sugar Icing: In a small mixing bowl combine 1 cup sifted *powdered sugar* and ¼ teaspoon *vanilla.* Stir in enough *milk* (2 to 4 teaspoons) to make an icing of drizzling consistency.

Nutrition information per serving: 338 calories, 4 g protein, 48 g carbohydrate, 15 g fat (2 g saturated), 53 mg cholesterol, 56 mg sodium.

Banana Split Cake

Looking for a star dessert for your next gathering? This one wins rave reviews for its soda fountain flavors.

1 package 2-layer-size banana
   cake mix
   Sweetened Whipped Cream or
   6 ounces frozen whipped dessert
   topping, thawed
1 cup sliced strawberries
1 8¼-ounce can crushed pineapple,
   well drained
1 11- to 12-ounce jar fudge ice-cream
   topping
½ cup coarsely chopped peanuts
   Banana slices (optional)

Prepare the banana cake mix according to package directions for a two-layer cake. Cool completely.

For fillings, divide the Sweetened Whipped Cream or dessert topping in half. Fold strawberries into half of the whipped cream. Fold drained pineapple into the remaining whipped cream. In a small saucepan heat and stir fudge topping over low heat just until warm (not hot).

To assemble, using a serrated knife, split each cake layer in half horizontally. Place bottom of 1 split layer on serving plate. Top with the strawberry filling, spreading to edge of layer. Top with another split layer. Spread with half of the fudge topping, letting some drizzle down side. Sprinkle with half of the nuts.

Top with another split layer. Spread with pineapple filling. Top with remaining split layer. Spread with remaining fudge topping, letting some drizzle down side of cake. Sprinkle with the remaining nuts.

Serve the cake immediately. (Or, cover loosely with plastic wrap, placing a few toothpicks in top of cake so wrap doesn't stick to topping, and chill up to 2 hours.) If desired, garnish the cake with banana slices. Makes 12 servings.

Sweetened Whipped Cream: In a chilled medium mixing bowl combine 1 cup *whipping cream*, 2 tablespoons *sugar*, and ½ teaspoon *vanilla*. Beat with an electric mixer on medium to high speed until soft peaks form (tips curl).

Nutrition information per serving: 494 calories, 7 g protein, 67 g carbohydrate, 24 g fat (10 g saturated), 63 mg cholesterol, 222 mg sodium.

Chocolate Cream Cake

This trio of devil's food layers is first filled with vanilla butter cream, and then the entire cake is swirled with chocolaty cream cheese frosting—an irresistible combination!

2⅔ cups all-purpose flour
1½ teaspoons baking soda
¾ teaspoon salt
¾ cup butter
2¼ cups granulated sugar
2 teaspoons vanilla
3 eggs
3 ounces unsweetened chocolate, melted and cooled
1½ cups ice water
Butter Cream Filling
Chocolate-Cream Cheese Frosting

Grease and lightly flour three 9x1½- or 8x1½-inch round baking pans. Combine flour, baking soda, and salt.

In a large mixing bowl beat the butter with an electric mixer on medium to high speed for 30 seconds. Add 2¼ cups sugar and vanilla; beat until combined. Add eggs, one at a time, beating well after each. Beat in melted chocolate. Alternately add flour mixture and water, beating on low to medium speed after each addition just until combined. Pour batter into prepared pans.

Bake in a 350° oven for 25 to 30 minutes or until a wooden toothpick inserted near the centers comes out clean. Cool in pans on wire racks for 10 minutes. Remove from pans. Cool completely on wire racks.

Spread Butter Cream Filling on two of the layers; stack layers. Top with remaining layer. Frost cake with Chocolate-Cream Cheese Frosting. Store, covered, in the refrigerator. Makes 12 servings.

Butter Cream Filling: Beat ½ cup *butter* until softened. Beat in 2¼ cups sifted *powdered sugar,* 2 tablespoons *milk,* and ½ teaspoon *vanilla.* Beat in additional *milk,* if necessary, to make a filling of spreading consistency.

Chocolate-Cream Cheese Frosting: Beat ½ of an 8-ounce package *cream cheese* until softened. Beat in 3 tablespoons *milk.* Beat in 3¾ cups sifted *powdered sugar.* Beat in 3 ounces *unsweetened chocolate,* melted and cooled, and 1 teaspoon *vanilla.* Beat in additional *milk,* if necessary, to make a frosting of spreading consistency.

Nutrition information per serving: 730 calories, 7 g protein, 113 g carbohydrate, 32 g fat (17 g saturated), 115 mg cholesterol, 564 mg sodium.

Desserts

Contents

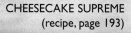

CHEESECAKE SUPREME
(recipe, page 193)

Country Pear and Cherry Crisp

Country Pear and Cherry Crisp

The topping stays extra-crunchy, and the best part is that it's a simple combination of granola and butter.

1   16-ounce package frozen unsweetened pitted tart red cherries, thawed, or one 16-ounce can pitted tart red cherries (water pack)
⅓   to ½ cup sugar
2   tablespoons all-purpose flour
1   teaspoon finely shredded orange peel
½   teaspoon ground cinnamon
3   to 4 medium pears, peeled, cored, and thinly sliced (3 cups)
1½ cups granola
2   tablespoons butter, melted
    Vanilla ice cream (optional)

If using canned cherries, drain cherries, reserving ½ cup juice. In a large mixing bowl combine frozen or canned cherries and reserved juice. Add sugar and toss to coat. Let stand for 5 minutes.

Combine flour, orange peel, and cinnamon. Sprinkle over cherries; toss to mix. Add pears; toss to mix. Transfer to an ungreased 2-quart square baking dish. Combine granola and butter; sprinkle over filling.

Bake in a 375° oven about 30 minutes or until pears are tender. If necessary, cover with foil the last 5 to 10 minutes to prevent overbrowning. Serve warm. If desired, serve with ice cream. Makes 6 servings.

Nutrition information per serving: 318 calories, 4 g protein, 58 g carbohydrate, 10 g fat (4 g saturated), 5 mg cholesterol, 94 mg sodium.

Red Wine-Marinated Peaches

Embellish this golden fruit with red wine, cinnamon, and cloves.

6   ripe medium peaches, peeled, pitted, and sliced, or pears, cored and sliced
1½ cups fruity red wine (such as Beaujolais) or dry white wine
¾   cup sugar
½   teaspoon ground cinnamon
⅛   teaspoon ground cloves

Place peaches or pears in a large bowl. For marinade, in a medium saucepan combine the wine, sugar, cinnamon, and cloves. Cook and stir over medium heat until sugar is dissolved.

Pour the marinade over peaches; toss gently to coat. Marinate at room temperature for 30 to 60 minutes, stirring occasionally. To serve, spoon the peaches and the marinade into dessert dishes. Makes 6 servings.

Nutrition information per serving: 262 calories, 1 g protein, 51 g carbohydrate, 0 g fat (0 g saturated), 0 mg cholesterol, 6 mg sodium.

Gingered Melon

Enjoy this cool, refreshing melon cup on the hottest days of summer.

¾	cup water
½	cup sugar
2	teaspoons finely shredded lemon peel (set aside)
4	teaspoons lemon juice
1½ to 2	teaspoons grated gingerroot
4	cups watermelon, cantaloupe, and/or honeydew melon balls
⅓	cup flaked coconut

For syrup, in a small saucepan combine water, sugar, lemon juice, and gingerroot. Bring to boiling; reduce heat. Simmer, uncovered, for 3 minutes. Remove from heat; stir in lemon peel. Cool to room temperature. If desired, strain syrup. Pour over melon. Stir gently to coat. Cover and chill for 2 to 24 hours.

To serve, spoon melon and syrup into dessert dishes. Sprinkle with coconut. Makes 6 servings.

Nutrition information per serving: 122 calories, 1 g protein, 28 g carbohydrate, 2 g fat (1 g saturated), 0 mg cholesterol, 10 mg sodium.

Honey-Fruit Pizza

Pretty as a picture, this fresh-tasting masterpiece features a cookie crust, summer fruits, and a honey glaze.

¾	cup butter
⅓	cup sifted powdered sugar
2	cups all-purpose flour
2	tablespoons honey
1	tablespoon cornstarch
⅓	cup apple or orange juice
2	tablespoons currant or apple jelly
1	cup sliced strawberries
1	medium nectarine, pitted and sliced, or 1 medium peach, peeled, pitted, and sliced
½	cup blueberries or raspberries
½	cup seedless green or red grapes, halved

For crust, beat butter with an electric mixer on medium speed for 30 seconds. Beat in the powdered sugar. Gradually add flour, beating until well mixed. Pat into a greased 11- or 12-inch pizza pan. Bake in a 375° oven for 15 to 18 minutes or until crust is golden brown. Cool in pan on a wire rack.

For glaze, stir together honey and cornstarch. Stir in juice and jelly. Cook and stir until thickened and bubbly. Cook and stir for 2 minutes more. Remove from heat. Cool for 5 minutes (do not stir). Spread half of the glaze over crust. Top with fruit and the remaining glaze. Chill at least 30 minutes before serving. Makes 12 servings.

Nutrition information per serving: 223 calories, 2 g protein, 28 g carbohydrate, 12 g fat (7 g saturated), 31 mg cholesterol, 118 mg sodium.

Gingered Melon

Chocolate-Irish Cream Cheesecake

Impress your guests with this home-baked version of a favorite often found on dessert carts in fine restaurants.

1 cup finely crushed chocolate wafers (about 17 cookies)*
¼ cup butter or margarine, melted
½ teaspoon ground cinnamon
3 8-ounce packages cream cheese, softened
1 8-ounce carton dairy sour cream
1 8-ounce package semisweet chocolate, melted and cooled
1 cup sugar
3 eggs
½ cup Irish cream liqueur**
2 tablespoons whipping cream or milk
2 teaspoons vanilla
⅓ cup semisweet chocolate pieces, melted (optional)

For crust, in a small bowl combine crushed wafers, butter or margarine, and cinnamon. Press mixture onto the bottom of an ungreased 9- or 10-inch* springform pan. Set aside.

For filling, in a large bowl beat cream cheese, sour cream, the 8 ounces melted chocolate, and sugar with an electric mixer on medium to high speed until smooth. Add eggs all at once. Beat on low speed just until combined. Stir in liqueur, cream or milk, and vanilla.

Pour into prepared pan. Place springform pan in a shallow baking pan. Bake in a 325° oven for 50 to 60 minutes or until center appears nearly set when shaken.

Cool in springform pan on a wire rack for 15 minutes. Loosen the cheesecake from side of pan; cool for 30 minutes more. Remove side of pan; cool for 1 hour. Cover and chill for 4 to 24 hours. To serve, if desired, drizzle cheesecake with the ⅓ cup melted chocolate. Makes 12 to 16 servings.

*Note: If using a 10-inch springform pan, use 1¼ cups crushed chocolate wafers for the crust.

**Note: If you prefer to use less liqueur, substitute whipping cream or milk for some of the liqueur.

Nutrition information per serving: 525 calories, 7 g protein, 34 g carbohydrate, 37 g fat (20 g saturated), 134 mg cholesterol, 295 mg sodium.

Cheesecake Supreme

Check for doneness by gently shaking the pan rather than inserting a knife, which will make a crack. When the cheesecake is done, a 1-inch area in the center will jiggle a little: this area will firm after cooling.

1¾ cups finely crushed graham crackers
¼ cup finely chopped walnuts
½ teaspoon ground cinnamon
½ cup butter or margarine, melted
2 8-ounce packages cream cheese, softened
1 cup sugar
2 tablespoons all-purpose flour
1 teaspoon vanilla
½ teaspoon finely shredded lemon peel (optional)
2 eggs
1 egg yolk
¼ cup milk
Raspberries (optional)
Raspberry Sauce (optional)

For crust, combine the graham crackers, walnuts, and cinnamon. Stir in butter or margarine. If desired, reserve ¼ cup of the crumb mixture for topping. Press the remaining crumb mixture onto the bottom and about 2 inches up the side of an 8- or 9-inch springform pan.

For filling, in a large mixing bowl beat cream cheese, sugar, flour, vanilla, and, if desired, lemon peel with an electric mixer on low speed until combined. Add eggs and egg yolk all at once. Beat on low speed just until combined. Stir in milk. Pour into the prepared pan. If desired, sprinkle with the reserved crumbs.

Place springform pan in a shallow baking pan. Bake in a 375° oven for 45 to 50 minutes for the 8-inch pan (35 to 40 minutes for the 9-inch pan) or until center appears nearly set when shaken.

Cool in pan on a wire rack for 15 minutes. Loosen crust from pan. Cool for 30 minutes more. Remove side of pan. Cool completely. Cover and chill at least 4 hours. If desired, garnish with raspberries and serve with Raspberry Sauce. Makes 12 to 16 servings.

Raspberry Sauce: In a blender container cover and blend 3 cups fresh or thawed, frozen *raspberries* (do not drain), half at a time, until smooth. Press berries through a sieve; discard seeds. In a saucepan combine ⅓ cup *sugar* and 1 teaspoon *cornstarch*. Add sieved berries. Cook and stir until thickened and bubbly. Cook and stir for 2 minutes more. Cool. Makes about 1 cup.

Nutrition information per serving: 429 calories, 7 g protein, 30 g carbohydrate, 32 g fat (18 g saturated), 137 mg cholesterol, 329 mg sodium.

No-Peel Apple Pie

The expression "easy-as-pie" surely applies to this home-style treat. Pick a thin-skinned apple, such as Golden Delicious, Jonagold, or Jonathan, to make it.

1 15-ounce package (2 crusts) folded
   refrigerated unbaked piecrust
6 large cooking apples
½ cup water
2 tablespoons lemon juice
½ cup granulated sugar
2 tablespoons all-purpose flour
1½ teaspoons apple pie spice
   Whipping cream or milk
   Coarse and/or granulated sugar

Let refrigerated piecrust stand at room temperature according to package directions. Unfold the piecrust. Ease one crust into a 9-inch pie plate. Set aside.

For filling, core and slice unpeeled apples (you should have 8 cups). In a large mixing bowl combine the apples, water, and lemon juice. Toss gently to coat. In another large mixing bowl stir together the ½ cup sugar, flour, and apple pie spice. Drain the apples well; add to sugar mixture. Toss gently to coat.

Transfer the filling to the pastry-lined pie plate. Trim pastry even with edge of pie plate. Cut out desired small shapes from center of the remaining piecrust. Set cutouts aside.

Place piecrust on top of filling; trim to ½ inch beyond edge of pie plate. Fold the top pastry under bottom pastry. Seal and flute edge. Cover edge with foil. Brush the pastry with a little whipping cream or milk. Top with pastry cutouts. Brush again with cream or milk. Sprinkle with coarse and/or granulated sugar.

Bake in a 375° oven for 30 minutes. Remove foil. Bake about 30 minutes more or until crust is golden brown. Cool slightly on a wire rack. Serve warm. Makes 8 servings.

Nutrition information per serving: 373 calories, 2 g protein, 58 g carbohydrate, 16 g fat (1 g saturated), 18 mg cholesterol, 211 mg sodium.

Pumpkin Pecan Pie

Filled with lots of crunchy pecans, this special dessert will become a must at your Thanksgiving celebration.

3 slightly beaten eggs
1 15-ounce can pumpkin
¾ cup sugar
½ cup dark-colored corn syrup
1 teaspoon vanilla
¾ teaspoon ground cinnamon
1 unbaked 9-inch piecrust
1 cup chopped pecans
Whipped cream (optional)
Ground cinnamon (optional)

In a medium mixing bowl combine eggs, pumpkin, sugar, corn syrup, vanilla, and ¾ teaspoon cinnamon; mix well. Pour into piecrust. Sprinkle with pecans.

Bake in a 350° oven for 50 to 55 minutes or until a knife inserted near center comes out clean. Cool on a wire rack. Refrigerate within 2 hours; cover for longer storage. If desired, serve pie with whipped cream and sprinkle with additional cinnamon. Makes 8 servings.

Nutrition information per serving: 412 calories, 6 g protein, 55 g carbohydrate, 20 g fat (4 g saturated), 80 mg cholesterol, 108 mg sodium.

Rice Pudding

This creamy rice pudding is a soothing conclusion to a spicy meal.

½ cup golden raisins	In a small bowl combine raisins and rum. Set aside. In a heavy medium saucepan combine milk, uncooked rice, and stick cinnamon. Bring to boiling; reduce heat. Cover and simmer about 20 minutes or until rice is tender. Remove stick cinnamon.
¼ cup rum	
3 cups milk	
½ cup long grain rice	
3 inches stick cinnamon	
¼ cup sugar	Drain the raisins, discarding rum. Stir the raisins, sugar, and vanilla into rice mixture. Sprinkle with ground cinnamon. Serve warm or chilled. Makes 6 servings.
1 teaspoon vanilla	
Ground cinnamon	

Nutrition information per serving: 200 calories, 6 g protein, 38 g carbohydrate, 3 g fat (2 g saturated), 9 mg cholesterol, 64 mg sodium.

Brownie Pudding

As this homey dessert bakes, a layer of cake magically rises to the top, leaving a chocolaty sauce underneath.

1 cup all-purpose flour	Grease an 8x8x2-inch baking pan; set aside. In a medium mixing bowl stir together the flour, granulated sugar, 2 tablespoons cocoa powder, baking powder, and salt. Stir in the milk, cooking oil, and vanilla. Stir in walnuts.
¾ cup granulated sugar	
2 tablespoons unsweetened cocoa powder	
2 teaspoons baking powder	
¼ teaspoon salt	
½ cup milk	Pour into the prepared pan. In another medium bowl stir together brown sugar and ¼ cup cocoa powder. Stir in the boiling water; slowly pour over batter. Bake in a 350° oven for 40 minutes. Cool on a wire rack for 45 to 60 minutes. Serve warm. Makes 6 to 8 servings.
2 tablespoons cooking oil	
1 teaspoon vanilla	
½ cup chopped walnuts	
¾ cup packed brown sugar	
¼ cup unsweetened cocoa powder	
1½ cups boiling water	

Nutrition information per serving: 368 calories, 5 g protein, 65 g carbohydrate, 12 g fat (2 g saturated), 2 mg cholesterol, 271 mg sodium.

Orange Bread Pudding with Warm Maple Sauce

So much flavor, so little fat—this bread pudding seemingly has it all.

4	slices white or whole wheat bread
⅓	cup raisins
3	eggs
2	egg whites
1¾	cups milk
⅓	cup orange marmalade
¼	cup sugar
½	teaspoon ground cinnamon
½	teaspoon vanilla
	Maple Sauce
	Orange slices, halved

Cut bread into 2-inch strips. Spread strips in a large shallow baking pan. Bake in a 325° oven for 10 to 15 minutes or until dry, stirring twice. Transfer strips to an ungreased 8x1½-inch round baking pan. Sprinkle with raisins. Set aside.

In a medium mixing bowl beat together eggs, egg whites, milk, orange marmalade, sugar, cinnamon, and vanilla with a wire whisk, fork, or rotary beater. Pour over bread and raisins in pan.

Bake in the 325° oven about 55 minutes or until a knife inserted near the center comes out clean. Cool slightly on a wire rack. Serve the bread pudding warm with warm Maple Sauce and garnish with orange slices. Makes 6 servings.

Maple Sauce: In a small saucepan combine 1 tablespoon *cornstarch* and ¼ teaspoon finely shredded *orange peel.* Stir in ¾ cup *orange juice* and ⅓ cup *maple-flavored syrup.* Cook and stir until thickened and bubbly. Cook and stir for 2 minutes more. Remove from heat. Stir in 1 teaspoon *butter* or *margarine.* Makes about 1 cup.

Nutrition information per serving: 299 calories, 9 g protein, 56 g carbohydrate, 5 g fat (2 g saturated), 113 mg cholesterol, 187 mg sodium.

Cinnamon Meringues with Fruit

For crispy meringue shells, serve them right away. However, if you like softer, marshmallowlike shells, chill them for up to 2 hours before serving.

2 egg whites
½ teaspoon ground cinnamon
½ teaspoon vanilla
¼ teaspoon cream of tartar
½ cup sugar
2 cups sliced peeled peaches or sliced nectarines
2 tablespoons sugar
1 tablespoon cornstarch
2 cups fresh fruit (such as sliced peeled peaches or kiwifruit and/or sliced nectarines or strawberries)

For meringue shells, cover a baking sheet with plain brown paper (specially made for baking). Draw six 3-inch squares or six 3½-inch circles on the paper. In a small mixing bowl beat the egg whites, cinnamon, vanilla, and cream of tartar with an electric mixer on medium speed until soft peaks form. Gradually add the ½ cup sugar, beating on high speed until stiff peaks form and sugar is almost dissolved.

Spoon meringue mixture into a decorating bag fitted with a medium plain-round or star tip (about ¼-inch opening). Pipe shells onto the prepared baking sheet. (Or, using a spoon or a spatula, spread the meringue mixture over the squares or circles on the prepared baking sheet, building up sides to form shells.)

Bake in a 300° oven for 30 minutes. Turn off the heat and let meringue shells dry in the oven with the door closed for at least 1 hour. (Do not open oven.) Peel off paper.

For sauce, place 2 cups peaches or nectarines in a blender container or food processor bowl. Cover and blend or process until nearly smooth. Pour into a saucepan. Mix 2 tablespoons sugar and cornstarch; stir into peach mixture. Cook and stir until thickened and bubbly. Cook and stir for 2 minutes more.

To serve, place meringue shells on dessert plates. Spoon the sauce into meringue shells. Top with fresh fruit. Serve immediately or cover and chill up to 2 hours. Makes 6 servings.

Nutrition information per serving: 138 calories, 2 g protein, 34 g carbohydrate, 0 g fat (0 g saturated), 0 mg cholesterol, 19 mg sodium.

Frosty Chocolate-Cherry Yogurt

Yogurt swirled with cherries and chocolate makes a cool, creamy, and scrumptious alternative to ice cream.

2   16-ounce cartons (3½ cups) vanilla
     yogurt (no gelatin added)*
2½ cups fresh or frozen pitted dark
     sweet cherries
⅓   cup milk
⅓   cup light-colored corn syrup
½   cup miniature semisweet
     chocolate pieces
     Fresh dark sweet cherries (optional)

In a blender container or food processor bowl combine yogurt, 1 cup of the pitted cherries, milk, and corn syrup. Cover and blend or process until mixture is almost smooth. (If using a food processor, process half at a time.)

Freeze in a 2-quart ice-cream freezer according to manufacturer's directions until almost firm. Add the remaining pitted cherries and chocolate. Continue to freeze as directed until firm. If desired, serve with additional fresh cherries. Makes 12 servings.

*Note: Yogurt without gelatin gives this dessert a better texture. Check the ingredients on the label.

Nutrition information per serving: 299 calories, 8 g protein, 55 g carbohydrate, 8 g fat (2 g saturated), 9 mg cholesterol, 107 mg sodium.

English Toffee Ice Cream

If you're making this frozen treat for kids, substitute milk for the coffee.

4   1.4-ounce bars chocolate-covered
     English toffee
2   cups whipping cream
1   14-ounce can sweetened
     condensed milk
½   cup strong coffee, cooled
1½ teaspoons vanilla

Crush toffee bars by placing them between two pieces of waxed paper and crushing them with a rolling pin. Set aside. Combine the whipping cream, sweetened condensed milk, coffee, and vanilla. Chill.

Beat with an electric mixer on low speed until slightly thickened. Fold in the crushed toffee. Spoon into a 2-quart square baking dish or a 9x5x3-inch loaf pan. Cover and freeze ice cream several hours or until firm. Makes 12 servings.

Nutrition information per serving: 315 calories, 4 g protein, 27 g carbohydrate, 21 g fat (12 g saturated), 68 mg cholesterol, 94 mg sodium.

Frosty Chocolate-Cherry Yogurt

CONTENTS

METRIC COOKING HINTS

By making a few conversions, cooks in Australia, Canada, and the United Kingdom can use the recipes in this book with confidence. The charts on this page provide a guide for converting measurements from the U.S. customary system, which is used throughout this book, to the imperial and metric systems. There also is a conversion table for oven temperatures to accommodate the differences in oven calibrations.

Product Differences: Most of the ingredients called for in the recipes in this book are available in English-speaking countries. However, some are known by different names. Here are some common U.S. American ingredients and their possible counterparts:

• Sugar is granulated or castor sugar.
• Powdered sugar is icing sugar.
• All-purpose flour is plain household flour or white flour. When self-rising flour is used in place of all-purpose flour in a recipe that calls for leavening, omit the leavening agent (baking soda or baking powder) and salt.
• Light-colored corn syrup is golden syrup.
• Cornstarch is cornflour.
• Baking soda is bicarbonate of soda.
• Vanilla is vanilla essence.
• Green, red, or yellow sweet peppers are capsicums.
• Golden raisins are sultanas.

Volume and Weight: U.S. Americans traditionally use cup measures for liquid and solid ingredients. The chart, above right, shows the approximate imperial and metric equivalents. If you are accustomed to weighing solid ingredients, the following approximate equivalents will help.
• 1 cup butter, castor sugar, or rice = 8 ounces = about 230 grams
• 1 cup flour = 4 ounces = about 115 grams
• 1 cup icing sugar = 5 ounces = about 140 grams

Spoon measures are used for smaller amounts of ingredients. Although the size of the tablespoon varies slightly in different countries, for practical purposes and for recipes in this book, a straight substitution is all that's necessary.

Measurements made using cups or spoons always should be level unless stated otherwise.

Metric Information
EQUIVALENTS: U.S. = AUSTRALIA/U.K.

$\frac{1}{5}$ teaspoon = 1 ml	$\frac{1}{2}$ cup = 120 ml
$\frac{1}{4}$ teaspoon = 1.25 ml	$\frac{2}{3}$ cup = 160 ml
$\frac{1}{2}$ teaspoon = 2.5 ml	$\frac{3}{4}$ cup = 180 ml
1 teaspoon = 5 ml	1 cup = 240 ml
1 tablespoon = 15 ml	2 cups = 475 ml
1 fluid ounce = 30 ml	1 quart = 1 liter
$\frac{1}{4}$ cup = 60 ml	$\frac{1}{2}$ inch = 1.25 cm
$\frac{1}{3}$ cup = 80 ml	1 inch = 2.5 cm

BAKING PAN SIZES

U.S. American	Metric
8x1½-inch round baking pan	20x4-cm cake tin
9x1½-inch round baking pan	23x4-cm cake tin
11x7x1½-inch baking pan	28x18x4-cm baking tin
13x9x2-inch baking pan	32x23x5-cm baking tin
2-quart rectangular baking dish	28x18x4-cm baking tin
15x10x1-inch baking pan	38x25.5x2.5-cm baking tin (Swiss roll tin)
9-inch pie plate	22x4- or 23x4-cm pie plate
7- or 8-inch springform pan	18- or 20-cm springform or loose-bottom cake tin
9x5x3-inch loaf pan	23x13x8-cm or 2-pound narrow loaf tin or pâté tin
1½-quart casserole	1.5-liter casserole
2-quart casserole	2-liter casserole

OVEN TEMPERATURE EQUIVALENTS

Fahrenheit Setting	Celsius Setting*	Gas Setting
300°F	150°C	Gas mark 2 (very low)
325°F	170°C	Gas mark 3 (low)
350°F	180°C	Gas mark 4 (moderate)
375°F	190°C	Gas mark 5 (moderately hot)
400°F	200°C	Gas mark 6 (hot)
425°F	220°C	Gas mark 7 (hot)
450°F	230°C	Gas mark 8 (very hot)
475°F	240°C	Gas mark 9 (very hot)
Broil		Grill

*Electric and gas ovens may be calibrated using Celsius. However, for an electric oven, increase the Celsius setting 10 to 20 degrees when cooking above 160°C. For convection or forced-air ovens (gas or electric), lower the temperature setting 10°C when cooking at all heat levels.